WHAT'S INSIDE HERE

This detailed book of clear, concise, short-form explanations is designed to create a basic understanding of the important Investing terms, concepts, and ideas for New and Beginner investors. The goal is to educate the reader so that they can have a solid basis from which to begin their Investing journey in financial markets.

The book consists of two independent sections, each emphasizing essential vocabulary and concepts.

SECTION 1: 55 Entries
FINANCE VOCABULARY FOR INVESTING

- General Finance
- Accounting
- Economics
- Management

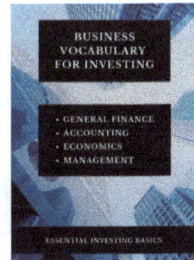

BUSINESS VOCABULARY FOR INVESTING

- GENERAL FINANCE
- ACCOUNTING
- ECONOMICS
- MANAGEMENT

ESSENTIAL INVESTING BASICS

SECTION 2: 195 Entries
INVESTING VOCABULARY

- Basic Investments
- Investment Analysis
- Trading & Strategy

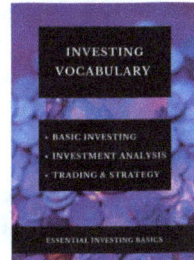

INVESTING VOCABULARY

- BASIC INVESTING
- INVESTMENT ANALYSIS
- TRADING & STRATEGY

ESSENTIAL INVESTING BASICS

INVESTING FOR BEGINNERS SERIES PART II:
"INVESTING TIPS TO LIVE BY"
Sold Separately on Amazon

Goldart Consulting LLC
(888) 203 - 6419
stuartg@goldartconsulting.com
www.goldartconsulting.com

FINANCE VOCABULARY FOR INVESTING

- GENERAL FINANCE
- ACCOUNTING
- ECONOMICS
- MANAGEMENT

ESSENTIAL INVESTING BASICS

1.

"TIME VALUE OF MONEY"

This is an important concept in the valuation of assets. Put simply, a dollar received today is worth more than a dollar received a year from now. Because if I receive a dollar today, at a minimum I can invest it in an interest bearing account and receive interest on it for a year. Therefore, in a year I will have my dollar plus some interest more. This is the Time Value of Money.

In business, even more options exist. A dollar received today can be invested in high-returning projects or could pay off high-rate credit card debts.

So when discussing terms with both vendors and customers, remember the maxim that a dollar today is worth more than a dollar tomorrow or a dollar next year, and use it to make decisions accordingly.

2.

"COMPOUNDING"

Compounding in business is the mathematical result that occurs when reinvestment is repeated over many periods of time. If it happens again and again over many years, the end result is exponentially grown as a function of the continued string of reinvestments.

An example: If we have $1,000 and we earn 10% each year. The first year, we received $100 in interest. When we add this to our initial money, we have $1,100. When we receive interest in the 2nd year, it will be $110, giving us a total of $1,210. In the 3rd year, we receive interest of $121 giving us $1,331. And so on.

This increasing interest effect, from $100 to $121 over two years is compounding.

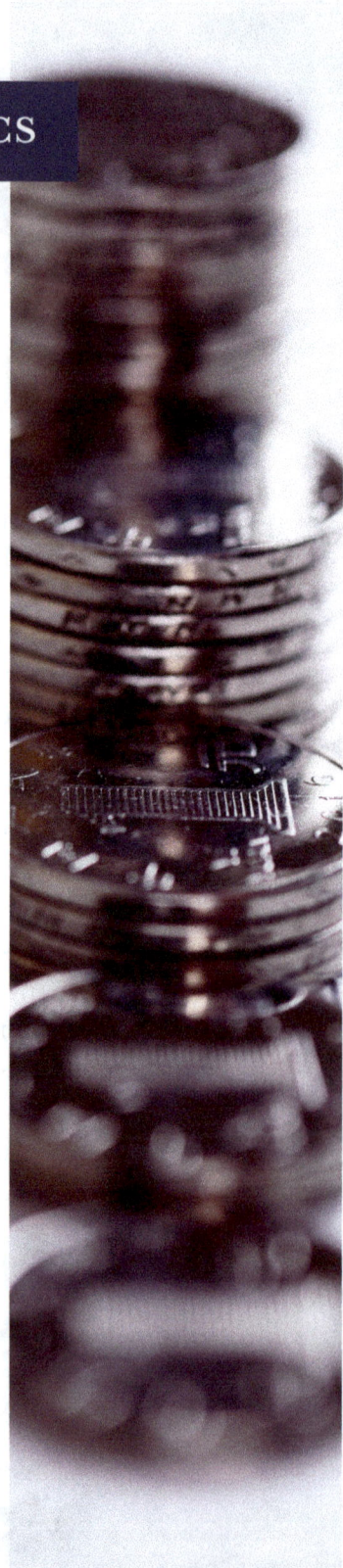

3.

"INTEREST / INTEREST RATE"

Interest is a financial element of a loan agreement, in essence, the price one pays for being able to take a loan. Interest is the rate of payment made for the pleasure of having that loan.

As an example, we can have a loan for $10,000 with an interest of 10%. Most loans come with an interest payment requirement, which means the borrower must pay a fee based on a declared rate multiplied times the total principle amount. In our scenario, 10% of $10,000, doing the math, is $1,000 in interest annually.

So in this scenario the total payments of Principal and Interest from borrower to lender is $11,000.

4.

"PRINCIPAL"

Principal is the total amount of money that is borrowed in the loan, thus it represents the money, not including interest, that needs to be paid back. It is important to remember that one will ultimately pay more than the Principal when one repays the loan (ie. the interest due).

As an example, we take a loan for $10,000 with an interest of 10%. Here the Principal amount is the $10,000, and that is the total amount that needs to be repaid if no interest is applied. However, most loans come with an interest payment requirement, which means the borrower must pay a fee based on a rate times the total principal amount.

So in this scenario the total payments of Principal and Interest from borrower to lender is $11,000.

5.

"OPPORTUNITY COST"

In business, we have limitations on certain assets such as Cash and Time. As such we need to make decisions on where to invest these most precious of assets. Since generally we cannot bet on all things at once, that means that certain opportunities will be pursued while others will not. From this state of affairs comes the idea of an Opportunity Cost.

Opportunity Cost is the price we pay for pursuing one activity while not pursing another. In theory, doing one activity precludes us from doing something else with our limited assets. So in business, we think of an opportunity lost and recognize that we want the activity we chose to create a greater return than the one we chose not to attempt.

7

6.

"LIQUID / ILLIQUID"

In Business, Liquid means how easily an asset can be turned into cash that can be used. Obviously that means that cash is the most liquid of assets. But other assets can be made liquid relatively quickly like publicly-traded stocks or a business's Accounts Receivable.

Illiquid Assets are those that cannot be easily turned into cash for use. A Picasso painting for instance is a valuable asset, but not very liquid.

Liquidity is also a measurement of how liquid a person's or a business's assets are. One is said to be Liquid when they have a sufficient level of liquid assets and the converse is true with illiquidity, not enough readily usable assets.

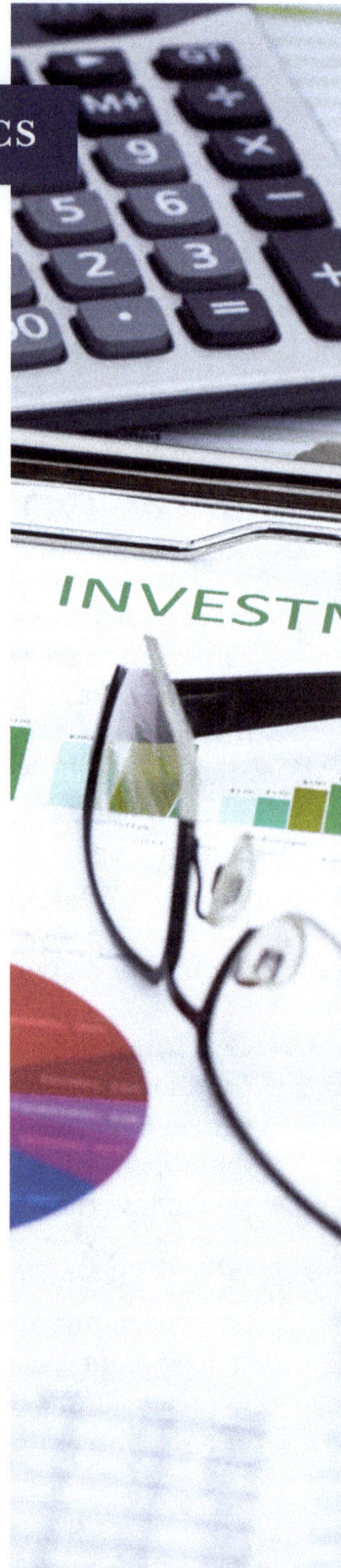

7.

"PRESENT VALUE"

When Finance people consider investments and the price they are willing to pay for some asset, they usually are evaluating the cashflows that the asset will bring over time. The concept of the Time Value of Money tells us that future cashflows are worth less than the cash received today.

So often potential investors or purchasers of assets will analyze future cashflows in what is known as their Present Value. This is calculated by "discounting" future cash flows into their value today, ie. Present Value. The calculation is a bit complex and depends on the rate of discounting and the time over which the discount occurs, but the concept is important in valuing investments. So remember, the Present Value of $1,000 received five years from now is worth less in today's dollars.

8.

"FUTURE VALUE

Similar to Present Value, yet in some senses its opposite, Future Value utilizes the concept of the time value of money to interpret the value in the future of some asset. The Future Value is largely based on the cash flows the asset generates over time based on an estimate of its compounded growth rate.

Again similar to a present value analysis, the calculation of a Future Value is complex. It takes into account a prevailing interest rate, usually the cost of capital, the time in the future being evaluated for and the cash flows expected. It is a corollary to the CAGR (discussed here elsewhere), but looks at a final dollar value number and not a growth rate percentage.

Many business valuations are often driven by Future Value estimations.

Return on Invest

Period Comparison

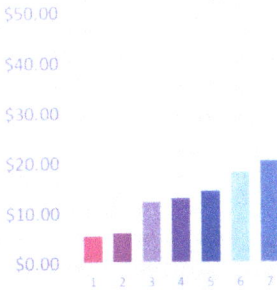

Item	Cost Per Item
1	$4.00
2	$5.00
3	$13.00
4	$11.50
	$10.00
6	$13.27
7	$14.51
8	$15.75
9	$17.00
10	$18.24
	$18.24
12	$20.72
13	
14	$22.56
15	$25.34
16	$26.72

Total

9.

"RISK - RETURN TRADE-OFF"

It is a core understanding in investments, and in life, that in order to take greater risk on something, there is a fair expectation of a greater return in reward for taking the risk. This is known as the Risk-Return Trade-off.

What is a sufficient return vis-à-vis a risk is independent and relative for each person and company. There are many factors that play into it, but in general in business, we should never take on greater risk if we are not going to be rewarded for that increased risk in terms of either some quantitative or qualitative measurement.

Spoken more plainly, taking on risk without a commensurate return is a bad decision.

11

10.

"RISK MANAGEMENT"

Risk Management is one of the preemptive responsibilities of senior management in a company. Some would say that Risk Management, managing the amount of risk in given situations and in the company as a whole, is the key role of a board of directors.

Companies manage risk by managing their cash flow, deciding which strategic projects to take on and which to pass on, and ensuring that proper management is in place to avoid improper decisions and actions. Such things as compliance departments and insurance policies are some of the tools companies use to manage risk. A strong combination of Corporate oversight and strategic analysis are essential elements to ensure a company can achieve its objectives in ethical and profitable manners.

11.

"ARBITRAGE"

Arbitrage is the concept of taking advantage of "price distortions" in a marketplace. While these distortions do not come very often, and are even less often capable of being exploited, from time to time they do exist and can lead to substantial profits.

An example: Imagine gold is selling in one country for $1,000 an ounce, and is selling in another country for $1,500 an ounce. It would be smart business to buy gold at $1,000 in the 1st country and immediately sell it at $1,500 in the 2nd country. This price distortion creates an arbitrage opportunity. In theory, enough people would do this arbitrage until the price in one country matches the price in the other country, and the opportunity disappears. Arbitrage is very hard to do with physical assets, but is more common with non-physical financial assets.

12.

"SUPPLY, DEMAND, SCARCITY, ABUNDANCE"

These powerful economic concepts have real life implications in all areas of business from sales and marketing to inventory management to Capital allocations. All goods and services that exist in a marketplace are affected by Supply (the amount available), Demand (the amount desired), and relative Scarcity and Abundance (imbalances between the other two, the first = deficiency and the second = excess).

In times of abundance or scarcity as a result of supply and demand imbalances, business managers will need to adjust strategies to account for that business landscape and its potential effect on their business.

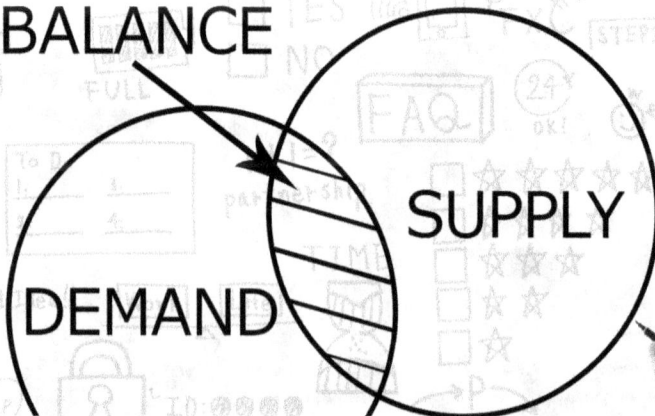

13.

"BOTTOMS-UP ANALYSIS"

Generally there are two different types of business analyses in terms of financial matters. Bottoms-Up Analysis is where the analysis is built from the most basic level of elements then driven upwards following the logic the analysis necessitates.

An example: A sneaker company needs to develop a forecast of its revenue. The Bottoms-Up Analysis builds the analysis by asking the question "What is the average price of the sneaker?" then asks how many sneakers is it estimated will be sold in a given period. These two are multiplied together to get the total revenue forecasted to be made for those sneakers in a given period.

Bottoms-Up Analysis forces the analyst to understand more deeply the individual elements of an analysis.

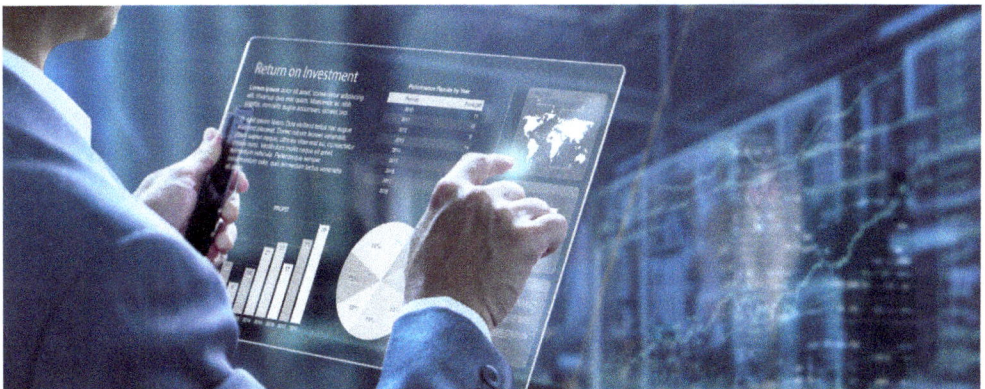

14.

"TOP-DOWN ANALYSIS"

The second type of financial analysis is called Top Down Analysis because the analyst choses a top figure first without analyzing any of the underlining elements that drive that figure.

An Example: In a Top-Down Analysis, if a sneaker company was asked to forecast its revenue for the coming year, it can merely choose the number $1 Million as the revenue for the year. The figure could be based on previous year's figures and an understanding overall of the elements that are projected to effect a total revenue number.

Top-Down Analysis is easier, but inferior to Bottoms-up analysis. But as it's both easier and faster to do, many Small Businesses use it.

15.

"DEBT SERVICE"

Debt Service, or servicing the debt, is when a business either returns principal and pays interest to people or institutions like banks who have lent them money. Those payments together, which are usually periodic and outlined in a loan agreement, are called Debt Service.

Servicing the debt is important, for if a company does not make the Debt Service payments that are outlined in the lending agreement, the company can be forced into bankruptcy by its lenders because of the non-payment. So it is essential that a company manage its cash flow in such a manner that it can service its outstanding debt, meaning, it can make regular principal and interest payments to its lenders, and thereby avoid bankruptcy.

16.

"NET REVENUE"

Net Revenue is the total revenue number produced subtracted by some amount. This is the general meaning of 'Net' in business, in that it removes some amount from a total. With Net Revenue, oftentimes it is Total Revenue minus a figure like returned sales or reimbursed expenses. Here, the total amount of returned sales is subtracted from the Total Revenue to get a Net Revenue figure.

The goal with calculating Net Revenue is to get to a truer figure about how a company is doing by subtracting out items that artificially inflate the Total Revenue figure. In some business scenarios, returns of sales can be very substantial with credits making up a significant percentage of Total Revenue. The Net Revenue figure is the more true figure for assessing sales success or disappointment in a period.

17.

"DILUTION"

Dilution is an important term in business as it concerns equity ownership in a company after a portion of the company has been sold. Much as adding water to some mixture will dilute the mixture, a similar principle occurs with financial Dilution, and stock ownership. Its importance pertaining to control of the company cannot be overestimated.

When an existing company sells a portion of its shares to a 3rd party, the current shareholders stake in the company is diluted. Example: If two people own 50% of a company and they sell 30% to an outside party, the percentages of the current shareholders is diluted. How this dilution occurs can affect how the company is managed and run. If they give up shares equally, both will only own 35% of the company, thus no longer having control of the company. If only one person gives up shares, the other person has control.

18.

"REVENUE, TOTAL & GROSS"

Revenue is the business term for Sales and is often used interchangeably with the word Sales. When we make a sale, that is giving someone or a business a good or service for a price, we create Revenue. Sales and Revenue are synonyms in a financial sense, with different companies and different industries using whichever of them is typical to that company or industry.

Total Revenue, also known as Gross Revenue, is the sum of all sales that are made in a given period. We calculate Gross Revenue by adding up all the sales of all the products and services sold, regardless of the type or nature of the good or service sold. One can calculate Gross Revenue of a given product or service, or one can calculate Total Revenue across a business.

REVENUE

19.

"LEVERED / LEVERAGE"

In Business, Leverage is the state of having debt in the business, and also it's a measurement of how much debt exists in a business's capital structure. It is called Leverage because having debt allows shareholders to expand the power of the shares they have in the company by borrowing money, and not selling away shares in the company (only 100% can exist).

With Leverage, and increasing levels of Leverage, a company becomes more risky because ultimately the company needs to pay back both the principal and the interest that the company has borrowed. Thus companies must watch and track carefully their Leverage ratios (calculations that measure company risk due to the amount of debt they have) and be sure to manage their cash flow appropriately to ensure Leverage does not put the company at risk of failure.

20.

"RECURRING REVENUE"

In some ways the dream of all businesses is Recurring Revenue, those revenue streams that occur monthly without much effort, input, or marketing activities.

Some classic examples are monthly fees like bank account fees and the monthly base charges on your cable or telephone bill. These expenses reoccur each month, oftentimes due to a contract signed by a customer and they reoccur again and again until the customer acts to stop that arrangement.

Large sums of monthly Recurring Revenue are often a path to great financial success and investor interest. One should always be looking to develop them.

21.

"EBITDA"

This acronym EBITDA stands for Earnings Before Interest, Taxes, Depreciation and Amortization. Many investors look at this metric of profitability as a significant sign of how the operations of a business are doing as it excludes elements that don't speak directly to the day-to-day operational running of the core fundamental business.

The elements listed in the acronym after Earnings are outside the core operations of the business. Taxes for example. While they are still quite essential to the success of the business, they do not speak to the basics of having a product and/or service that is trying to reach a market. So as a more uncluttered look on progress or success, many investors will focus on EBITDA because if this number is not positive or at least growing, it truly speaks to problems in the core situation.

22.

"NET INCOME"

Net Income is the final and most important profitability metric, especially for publicly-traded companies on stock exchanges. It represents profitability after all expenses are deducted from its gross margin including all fixed expenses, taxes, interest, depreciation and amortization.

Most very mature companies are judged by Net Income, which is oftentimes also called rather simply in short form, Earnings. Companies on a stock exchange are evaluated on a Net Income basis, and the most important metric existing for evaluating them is known as Earning per share, which is the total Net Income earnings in some given period, quarterly or annually, divided by the total number of shares outstanding.

23.

"DEBT"

Debt is the name business gives to monies owed to someone or some organization like a bank or other lending institution. Debt is a part of the Total Liabilities category. When a business takes a loan, either short-term or long or both, we collectively referred to this amount outstanding and needed to be repaid as Debt.

Debt is not necessarily a bad thing for a business to have, but too much of it is difficult to manage as eventually we have to pay back to the lender both the principal (the amount we borrowed) and interest on the principal. This can adversely effect the cash flow of a company especially if there is too much cash being utilized for payments.

So managing total Debt is essential for the long-term success of a business.

24.

"ASSETS"

To make it very simple, an Asset is something that has value. It is generally something that can be sold at some price to a buyer outside the company. The most classic examples of Assets in business are cash in a bank account, inventory of products, monies owed to the company in the form of a loan to someone or monies owed to the company for payment of sales to them (Accounts Receivable defined in coming pages).

Assets is one of the three main sections of the Balance Sheet financial statement. The ratio of assets to various things like liabilities or equity (defined on other pages here) are key metrics that investors and bankers use to decide on the credit or investing worthiness of a company.

25.

"LIABILITIES"

Somewhat different to the definition in regular life, Liabilities in business means that money is owed to someone or something. Liabilities is a broad category that can include credit card loans, long-term bank loans, bond payments to investors, and even monies owed to product or service providers called Accounts Payables.

Liabilities represents one of the three main sections of the Balance Sheet financial statement, and is a key figure in deciding the financial health of a company. Companies with too many liabilities as compared with their assets or equity are often in serious financial trouble and a risk for both lenders and providers to do business with.

26.

"OWNER'S EQUITY"

Owner's Equity is one of the main three sections of a Balance Sheet analysis, and it represents the value of the business at least as far as the Balance Sheet is concerned. It represents the Net worth of a business in its most basic form. It is calculated by subtracting the total liabilities of the company from the total assets of the company. The difference between the two is Owner's Equity.

Though some slight differences can exist in certain circumstances, essentially the terms Owner's Equity and Book Value are synonyms, and can be used interchangeably. Book Value is usually used in an investment context. Owner's Equity is generally used more in the context of accounting and tax filings.

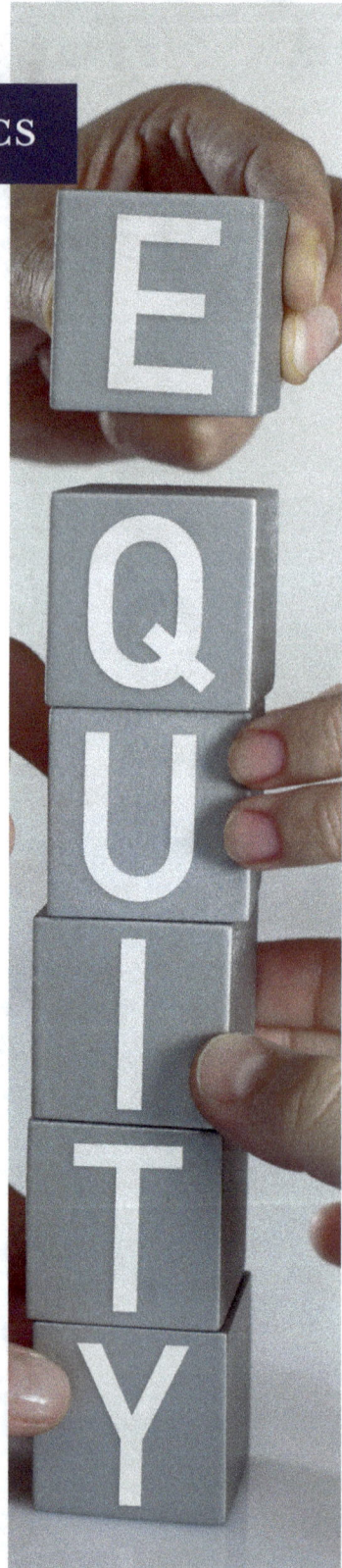

27.

"BOOK VALUE"

Book Value, for the most part, is another way of saying Owner's Equity. Thus it is defined similarly as the difference between the value of the assets as calculated on the Balance Sheet and the total liabilities. Hence its name, it's the value of the company "on the books."

It's important to understand that Book Value is a metric rarely used to value companies, and does not truly represent the value of a company for purchase or stock valuation purposes. Because most companies are worth more than their Book value as intangible assets like brand equity (defined elsewhere) can be worth even more than the Book value as calculated on the Balance sheet.

Think of the value of certain brands like Apple or Coke. The loyalty they inspire is almost invaluable, but it is not technically calculated in a Book Value analysis.

28.

"GOODWILL"

In business there are assets, and even whole companies, that are worth more than their listed book value calculated on the company's balance sheet. Goodwill is the name given to this "excess value" above the calculated book value.

The most common usage is the difference between the value of a company in the marketplace versus the book value of the company on the balance sheet. Book value is the difference in value between a company's assets minus its liabilities. The marketplace value of a company is defined by its total outstanding shares times its current stock price.

If a company's book value is $1 million, but its marketplace value is $3 million, the two million dollar difference between the two is Goodwill.

29.

THE 3 FINANCIAL STATEMENTS:
"INCOME STATEMENT"

Also known as the Profit and Loss Statement interchangeably, the Income Statement is one of the three major financial statements that all companies should or must produce, from your small company to Apple computer.

This statement captures the profitability (or loss) of the company over some specific defined period of time. An Income Statement can be for a month, a quarter, annually or any other designed period. This is in contrast with a Balance Sheet, which is capturing a specific point in time, say today or year-end.

While complicated, specifically, the format is a showing of revenue minus expenses which produces a profit-defining result for that period of time.

31

30.

THE 3 FINANCIAL STATEMENTS: "BALANCE SHEET"

The Balance Sheet of a company is one of three major financial statements that all companies produce. It is essentially a Net Worth analysis of a company, showing a value "on paper" of what a company is worth, as well as outlining other key performance indicators.

The main analysis is a comparison of the assets of the company to the liabilities of the company. The normal calculated difference between these two categories is known as Owner's Equity, which is a value of the company in a certain sense. In the equation, the assets of the company must equal the sum of the value of the Liabilities of the company plus its current Owner's equity.

ing values and the fair values of financial instrur

	Group		
	Carrying value £m	Fair value £m	Carrying value £m
s	6,121	6,121	4,759	4
	4,516	4,516	3,004	3
	975	975	2,534	2
	5,491	5,491	5,538	5
	52,736	52,736	44,965	44
or loss	376	376	282	
	29,494	29,474	25,340	25
	82,606	82,586	70,587	70
	462	72,462	53,9(	
	27	1,327	6	
	3	382,671	350,96	
	21	11,504	11,68	
6,893	467,964	417,226	
ofit or loss	95,192	95,192	80,653	
	5,989	5,989	3,991	
	25,509	25,509	35,533	
	561	561	788	
	127,251	127,251	120,965	
profit or loss	3,038	3,038	2,9	
	2,610	2,610	2,541	
	7,856	7,856	3,819	
	13,504	13,504	9,301	
	7,425	7,425	6,00	
	116,681	116,681	95,6(	

31.

THE 3 FINANCIAL STATEMENTS:
"THE CASH FLOW STATEMENT"

The least well-known of the main financial statements, but in some ways the most important, is the Cash Flow Statement, which tracks cash specifically.

In general, there are three ways a business generates cash. One is from its operations, the second is from investments made in assets outside the company, the third is cash from investments made into the company (AKA investors). This statement tracks the net effect, either positive or negative, of each driver of cash in the business.

Just the fact that this analysis is one of the main schedules completed for all business underscores how important cash is to businesses.

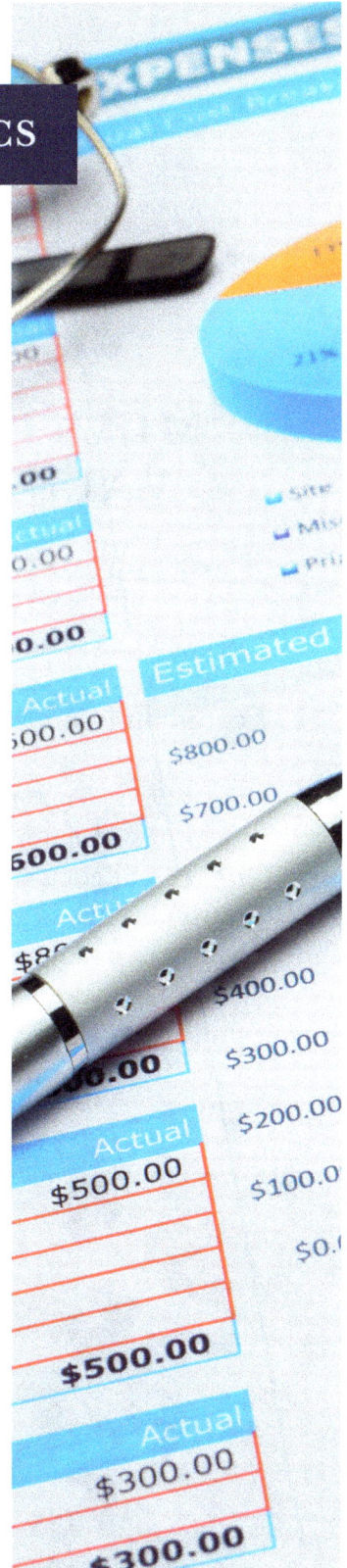

32.

"MULTIPLE-OF-EARNINGS VALUATION METHOD"

Essentially, there are three main ways that companies are valued when someone or some company is considering making an investment or purchasing outright an existing company. The easiest and most common is known as the Multiple of Earnings Method.

Simply, it is a matter of taking some metric of the earnings of a company and multiplying that by a some figure called a multiple. The multiple is most often a number that is standard within an industry. So if the average bank company is valued at 8 times its earnings, one takes the earnings of a bank to be valued and multiplies it times 8. Note: The metric of earnings may vary between industries and companies (Net Income, EBITDA, Net Revenue, Free Cashflow, etc.)

33.

"DISCOUNTED CASHFLOW (DCF) VALUATION METHOD"

The second most common way of evaluating a company for investment or outright buying is the Discounted Cashflow Method. It is much more difficult and complex than the Multiple of Earnings method thus less used.

In essence, an analysis is done that forecasts the cashflows that will come from a company over a period of time, often 10 years. Then these cashflows are "discounted" into their Present Value using an appropriate discount rate, which is often a prevailing interest rate or the cost of capital of a potential acquirer.

It can be difficult to forecast out accurately the cashflows of a company so this method has risks.

34.

"SUM-OF-THE-PARTS VALUATION"

The third main Valuation method of companies is known as the Sum-of-the-Parts method. This is generally used for large corporations that have various business lines and legal entities under the one conglomerated company.

Essentially giant companies are oftentimes really just several smaller companies under one umbrella. So to value the larger company, it is often advisable to try to evaluate each of the smaller parts then add up the values. This gives a sense of the value of the larger company as whole if was broken up into its smaller pieces. Hence the name, Sum of the Parts. Clearly, this only works for large companies with many different divisions or companies under one roof.

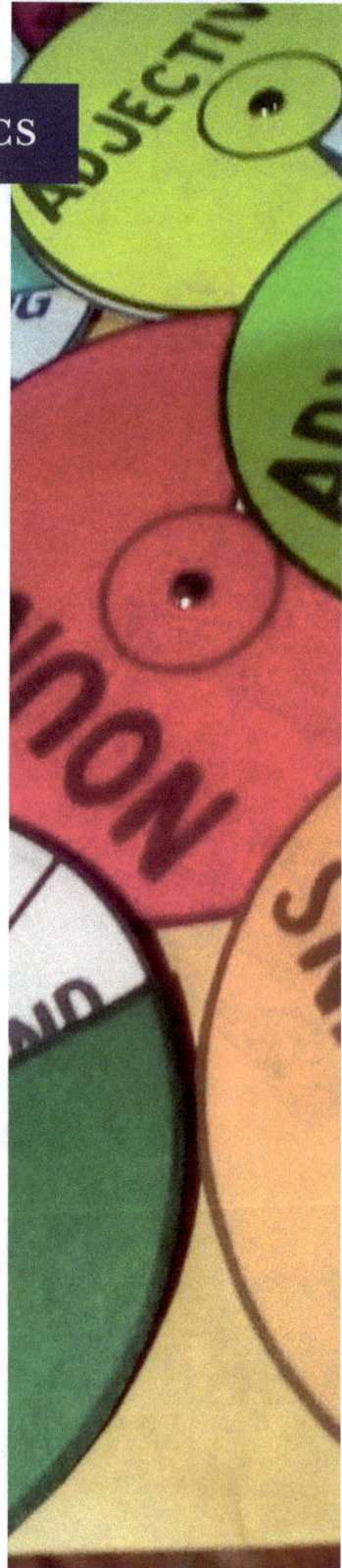

35.

"VOTING INTEREST / VOTING CONTROL"

With shares in a company, also known as stock or equity, it is generally arranged that one share equals one vote. So when one owns a share, one has a Voting Interest in the company.

However, it is possible to setup different classes of stock, and give one class of stock the power to have greater number of votes per share. Some companies have done either 10 or 20 votes per share with a special classes of shares.

When you have over 50% of the voting shares in a company, it is said that you have Voting Control. That is, on any corporate vote, you control the majority so in theory, the vote will go as you decide it given your majority stake.

36.

"ECONOMIC INTEREST / ECONOMIC CONTROL"

One has an Economic Interest in a company when one owns shares in a company. So if that company earns money or pays dividends, as the owners of shares, you will receive your percentage of the cashflows that the company distributes to its shareholders.

An example: I own 10% of a company so my economic interest in the company is 10%. If the company earns $1 Million in a given year and it votes to distribute those profits to its shareholders, my 10% economic interest will allow me to receive $100,000 as a result.

Economic Control is when a person owns more than a 50% of an Economic Interest in a company.

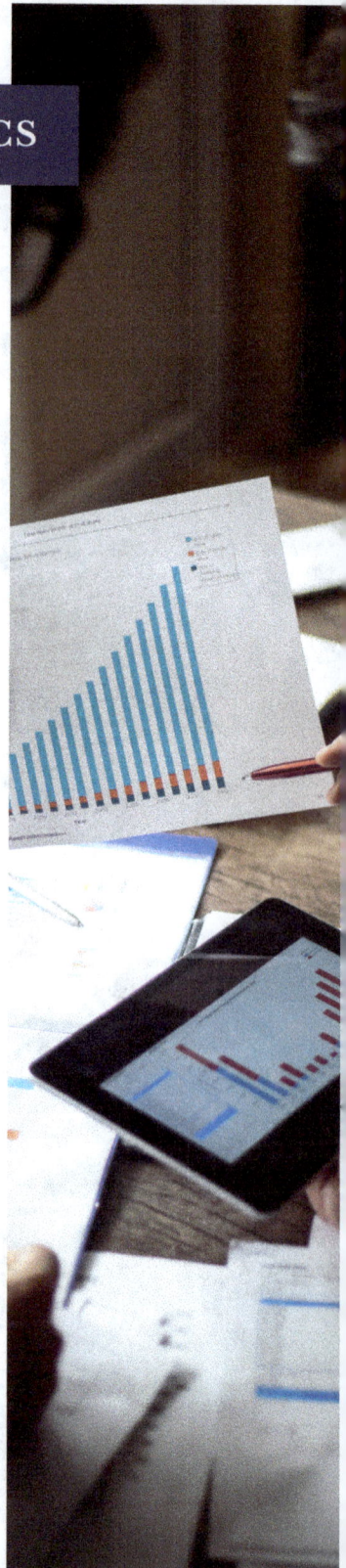

37.

"RETURN ON INVESTMENT (ROI)"

Businesses make investments in property, equipment, projects, and other companies with the hope of generating a Return on the Investment (ROI), that is more money returned than was invested, all factors considered. We call the extra money earned the Return on the Investment.

In Business, we calculate this amount in a different manner than we do in regular life. In Business we recognize that we have many opportunities to invest in and so there is an opportunity cost for making one investment over another. So when we make an investment, we take into account the cost of choosing this option so that for a return to be a good investment, it must return our money plus a rate greater than our opportunity cost, ie other choices.

38.

"FINANCIAL RATIOS"

Financial Ratios are a series of calculations that are designed to give an analyzer a sense of the status and health of a company. When the numbers are good, these ratios speak to the stability and success of the ongoing company. Conversely, when the numbers are poor, they speak to instability and lack of financial health.

The most common of the Financial Ratios include but are not limited to Coverage and Debt ratios, which speak to the company's ability to manage its debt. Also Efficiency ratios such Receivable and Inventory turnover which speak to a company's ability to effectively utilize its assets.

All together, Financial ratios can be an important tool to track health and progress over time.

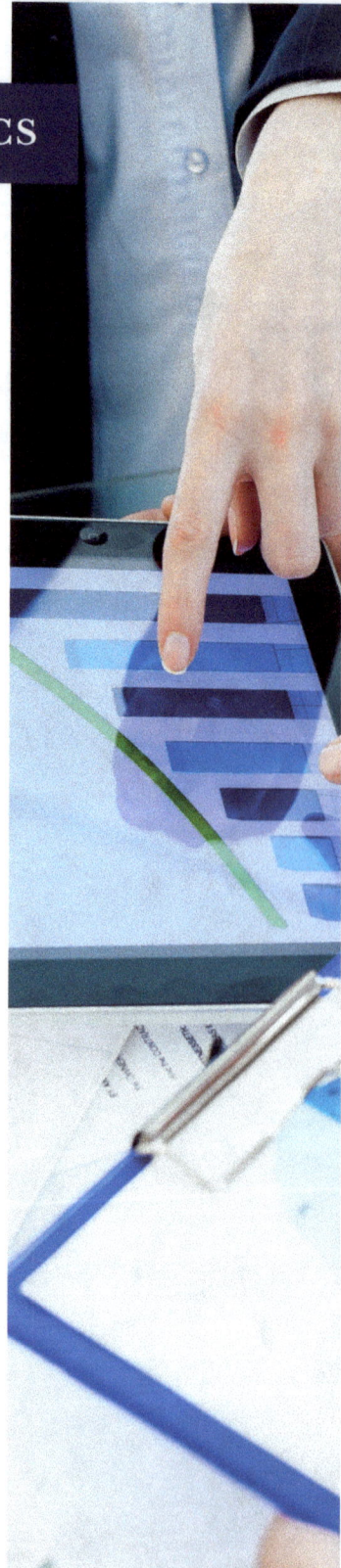

39.

"COMPOUNDED ANNUAL GROWTH RATE (CAGR)"

In Business, the rate of growth of earnings for a company is a very important metric that speaks to its financial health and future prospects. Investors take growth rates very seriously when considering whether to make an investment or buy stock as companies with higher growth rates generally produce greater returns to investors over time.

The Compounded Annual Growth Rate metric, known as CAGR in the financial industry, is a calculation that shows the growth rate of an item, usually earnings, but occasionally revenue or cash flow. It calculates the rate of growth taking into account compounding, which means the annual growth rate year over year. The calculation is quite difficult, but the concept is essential to understand.

40.

"FORWARD-LOOKING / SAFE HARBOR STATEMENTS"

Forward-Looking Statements, also known as Safe Harbor Statements, are those statements made by companies that cannot be proven by a past fact, and are in fact, statements about the future which the company is making but cannot be assumed or counted on to occur. Typical Forward-Looking Statements in business are all sorts of business forecasts such as revenue projections, profit and earnings forecasts, market share assumptions etc.

Companies in their securities filings and offering memorandum must mention that Forward-Looking Statements are being made so as to inform the reader (potential investor) that relying on these statements as facts is not correct, and that there is risk to relying on the statements given their unconfirmed nature.

41.

"BLUE SKY LAWS"

Blue Sky Laws are state laws intended to protect investors from fraud, specifically fraudulent claims made by those people and companies looking to raise capital from investors. Since they are State laws, they will vary by each state, though similarities exist among the different state Blue Sky Laws.

In essence, Blue Sky Laws require sellers of shares known as issuers to register their securities for sale and provide investors with various and sufficient information that the potential investor can use to better understand all of the risks and opportunities associated with a potential investment. They are intended to limit extreme claims (promising the Blue Sky) made by the issuer as pertains to the offering and create liabilities for the issuers if fraud is deemed to have occurred as pertains to fraudulent claims made.

42.

"E.S.G."

The acronym ESG stands for Environmental, Societal, and Corporate Governence, and together it is a school of thought speaking to and asking for responsible business activities in various areas of business procedures and investing. The areas often are concerned with issues such as global warming, drug and sex trafficking, child labor and underaged employment issues and other societal concerns.

Many companies now, especially investment companies, are developing strategies to ensure their business practices, and even investment choices, either reflect or are outright designed to ensure adherence to practices and policies that take what is believed to be a positive stance in societal matters.

43.

"STORE OF VALUE"

An asset is said to have a Store of Value when (1) it can priced, (2) have that price be relatively stable, and (3) be used as currency in some fashion for an exchange of goods. The most classic asset that acts as an example of a Store of Value is a common currency such as the United States dollar.

To explain further by way of an example, the United States dollar can be priced and is in a market every day, its price is relatively stable over time so parties can trust its value, and it can be used for an exchange of goods easily and readily.

By contrast, Bitcoin has no Store of Value because its price is not very stable so it would be foolish for people to use it in an exchange for goods. Its volatility makes it impossible to be a Store of Value.

44.

"SECURED/UNSECURED DEBT"

The debt a company has, ie., monies owed to either a person, business or institution, can be Secured or Unsecured. The difference between these two is whether some asset of the company has been pledged specifically against the money owed. This becomes very important if a company were to go bankrupt.

An example: A company has borrowed $20,000 from a bank and pledged a building purchased with the money against that loan. Now that loan (read: debt) is secured by the value of the building. If the company were to go bankrupt, the bank would have the right to sell the building to recoup the money on its loan.

Unsecured debt is not tied to any specific asset, and is much riskier as a result. The lender can only recoup money if there are leftover assets in the business.

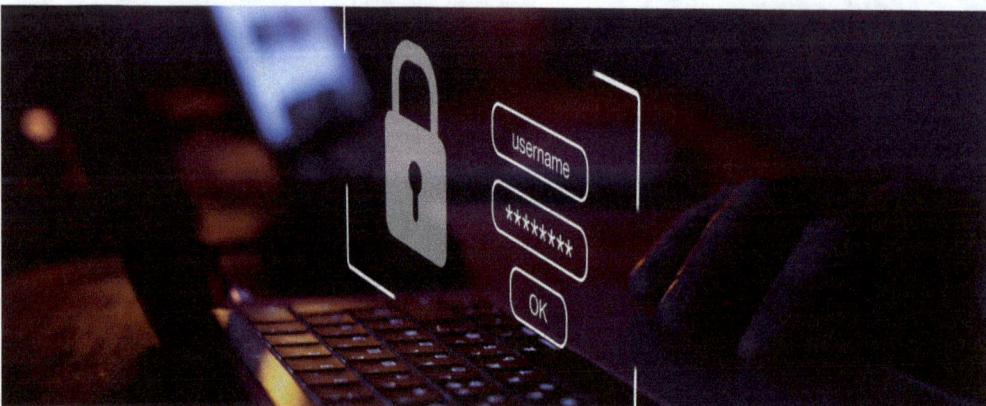

45.

"OPPORTUNITY COST"

In Business we have limitations on certain assets such as Cash and Time. As such we need to make decisions on where to invest these most precious of assets. Since generally we cannot bet on all things at once, that means that certain opportunities will be pursued while others will not. From this state of affairs comes the idea of an Opportunity Cost.

Opportunity Cost is the price we pay for pursuing one activity while not pursing another. In theory, doing one activity precludes us from doing something else with our limited assets. So in business, we think of an opportunity lost and recognize that we want the activity we chose to create a greater return than the one we chose not to attempt. Often we can calculate the opportunity cost and add that sum to the cost of the project chosen.

46.

"FINANCIAL RATIOS"

These are a series of calculations that are designed to give an analyzer a sense of the status of a company. When the numbers are good, these ratios speak to the health and stability of the company. Conversely, when the numbers are poor, they speak to instability and lack of financial health.

Common financial ratios include but are not limited to Coverage and Debt Ratios, which speak to the company's ability to manage its debt, and Efficiency Ratios which speak to a company's ability to effectively utilize its assets.

All together, Financial Ratios can be an important tool to track health and progress over time.

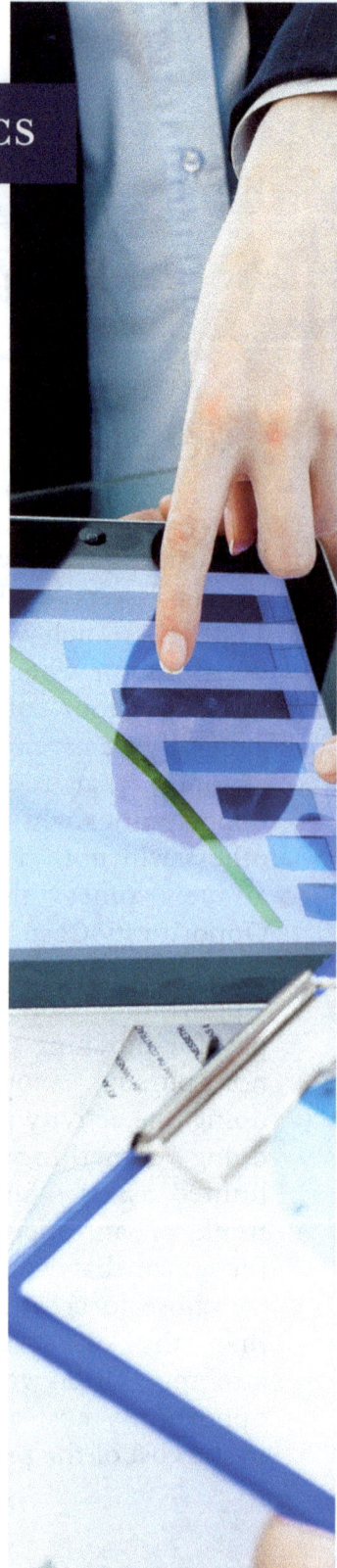

47.

"COVERAGE RATIOS"

A type of Financial Ratio, Coverage Ratios focus completely and specifically on a company's ability to handle its debt and debt service. In other words, if the company can make its Principal and Interest payments on a timely basis and with sufficient cash to continue to fund the operations of the business.

Generally, but not always, the calculation is a function of projected cash flow divided into some form of debt servicing payments. If cash flow is a high multiple of debt servicing payments, it means the company has plenty of ability to fulfill its commitments. If the the multiple is small or even worse, fractional, it means the company is in financial jeopardy.

48.

"CAPITAL STRUCTURE"

Capital Structure refers to how a company finances its business operations. The two elements that are used are Equity and Debt (previously defined). Most companies will use a combination of both elements to most effectively and efficiently finance the business.

If 70% of the capital a company uses to fund its operations comes from Equity sales and 30% comes from debt (loans, bonds) it is said that this company has a 70-30 Capital Structure.

For most companies, having more debt increases the risk associated with the company because it must make its Principal and Interest payments. But, companies with no debt are not taking enough risk to get a better return.

49.

"IMPUTED VALUE"

Imputed Value is a way of discerning the value of a whole company based on the sale of a portion of the company. It is a very important metric in fundraising.

If, for example, 10% of a company is sold to an investor for $50,000 (the Imputed Value) the value implied as a function of this transaction is $500,000. Likewise, if 33% of the company is sold for $1 million, the company is being valued at $3 million.

Oftentimes in fundraising, it is important to have an increasing valuation based on the imputed values of one's fundraising transactions, as it shows a company becoming more valuable in the marketplace.

50.

"INVENTORY"

Inventory is a term that describes the stockpiles of a company's specific products that it sells. Inventory can be spoken of as a company total, when a company offers several products for sale, or as an individual total of an individual product.

For example, Apple computers will have a total Inventory number, which represents the value of all its products in Inventory. It will also have an Inventory number for a specific product like iPhones, even calculated by each series of phones. Companies also may keep Inventory of raw materials and parts.

Inventory can be described either in total dollar terms or total unit terms depending what exactly one is looking to analyze. It can also include parts and supplies.

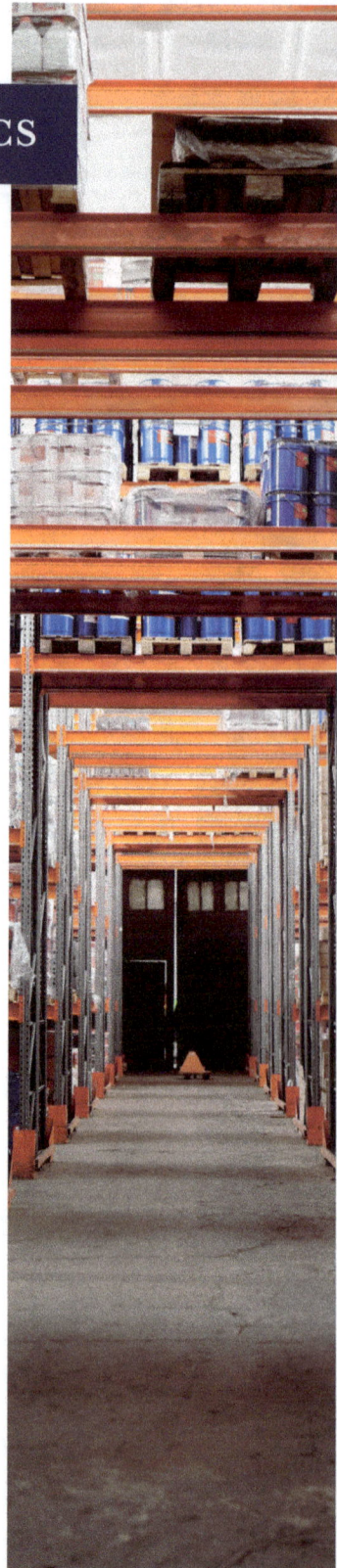

51.

"GOODWILL"

In business there are assets, and even whole companies, that are worth more than their book value carried on the company's balance sheet. Goodwill is the name given to the excess value above the calculated book value.

The most common usage is the difference between the value of a company in the marketplace versus the book value of the company on the balance sheet of the company. Book Value is the difference in value between a company's assets minus its Liabilities. The marketplace value of a company is defined by its total outstanding shares times its stock price.

If a company's Book Value is one million dollars, but its value in the marketplace is three million dollars, the two million dollar difference between the two is Goodwill.

52.

"GENERALLY ACCEPTED ACCOUNTING PRINCIPLES (GAAP)"

The basic accounting system used all over the world is known as the Double Entry Accounting system and it was reportedly created by monks in the 14th century. To ensure that all people who use the system use it in similar fashion, accounting industries have created a set of commonly understood rules and practices known as Generally Accepted Accounting Principles, usually known by the acronym GAAP.

In financial reporting for public companies, the principles of GAAP accounting govern how companies account and report the financial results.

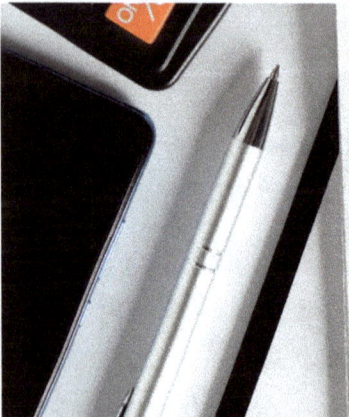

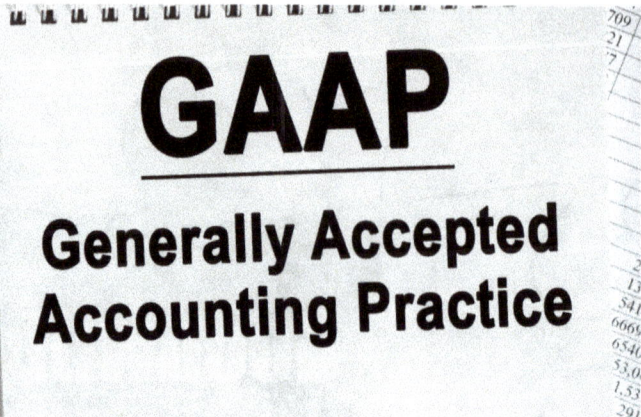

53.

"THE ACCOUNTING EQUATION"

The basic formulation that undergirds all of the Double Entry Accounting system is known as The Accounting Equation and it is as follows:

Assets - Liabilities = Owner's Equity

It is sometimes shuffled around to where Assets are alone on one side of the equation, but that is the same thing just reformulated. It can be adjusted even further to have Liabilities be the summation. Irrespective The Accounting Equation always says the same thing. Essentially, what we have minus what we owe is what we are worth.

Assets -
Liabilities =
Equity

54.

"RETAINED EARNINGS"

Generally one of the more complicated of the accounting elements registered on financial statements, Retained Earnings is confusing as people often think of it as a pile of cash given its name, when in fact, it is more of an accounting construct. It represents the amount of profits leftover for business purposes.

Retained Earnings are those earnings that a company produces, but does not divest to shareholders. It is a figure that grows year after year if the company is profitable, or conversely decreases if the company is not. Again Retained Earnings do not represent a large sum of cash to be deployed or divested, it is an accumulation of profits not divested over time, hence retained.

55.

"SALES TAX / VALUE ADDED TAX"

In most but not all jurisdictions (city, state, & federal), there is a tax placed on End sales made within that jurisdiction. These Sales Taxes are paid by the customer buying a finished product. The company must capture the Sales Tax for future submission to the appropriate tax authority.

It is essential that small businesses collect the Sales Tax, account for them on their books, and ultimately submit the tax (cash) to the jurisdiction. Failure to do so is tax fraud, and can result in huge penalties and even jail time.

Certain countries use a Value Added Tax, which taxes product sales each step of the way in production versus just taxing one time at the sale of the end product.

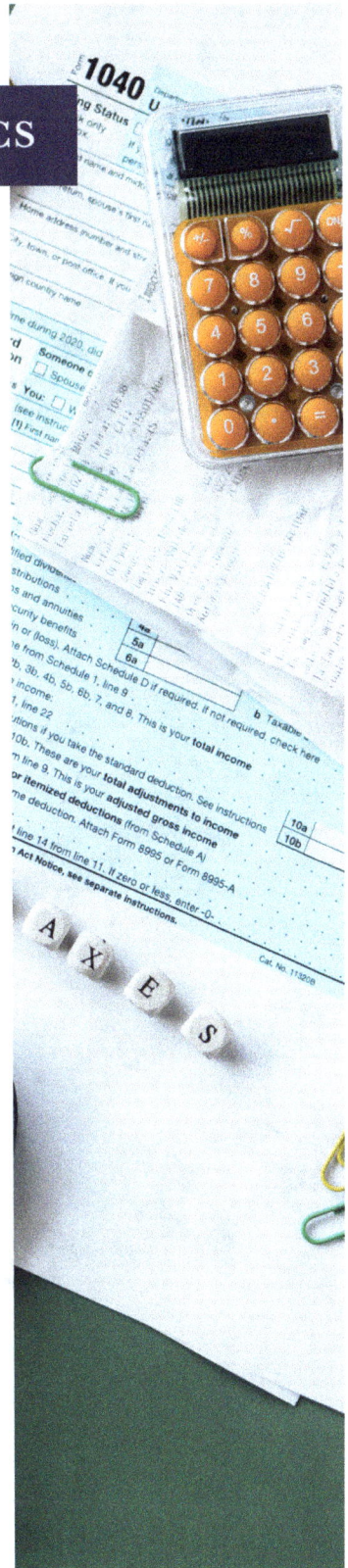

INVESTING VOCABULARY

- **BASIC INVESTING**
- **INVESTMENT ANALYSIS**
- **TRADING & STRATEGY**

ESSENTIAL INVESTING BASICS

INVESTING VOCABULARY

BASIC INVESTING

ESSENTIAL INVESTING BASICS

1.

"STOCK / SHARES"

Stock, and in plural, stocks also known as shares, are ownership units in a company. Each unit represents a portion of the ownership. So if you own any stock or shares in a company, you're an owner of the company, be it a local laundromat or Apple Inc.

Obviously, one's ownership percentage is a function of the number of shares one owns, as divided by the total number of outstanding shares. As you can imagine, owning 10 shares of Apple Computer gives you a very miniscule ownership percentage of Apple, while ten shares of the local laundromat, which may only have a 100 shares outstanding, will give you a 10% ownership stake in that entire company.

But an owner is an owner, no matter how big or small, and stock/shares are the representation of an ownership percentage.

2.

"EQUITY"

Equity is really just a fancy name for stock ownership in finance. Be it in the stock market, collectively known as Equities, or in a single company called Equity or an equity holding. It represents that someone possesses an ownership percentage in a company.

Sometimes it is expressed in the number of shares owned (say, 30 or 3,000 shares), and sometimes it is expressed in a percentage ownership of a company (2% or 100% etc.). There is no limitation on the number of shares one can own, but 100% is the maximum percentage we can own.

Equity is different from Owner's Equity in that, though both speak to ownership value, the second is an accounting figure primarily.

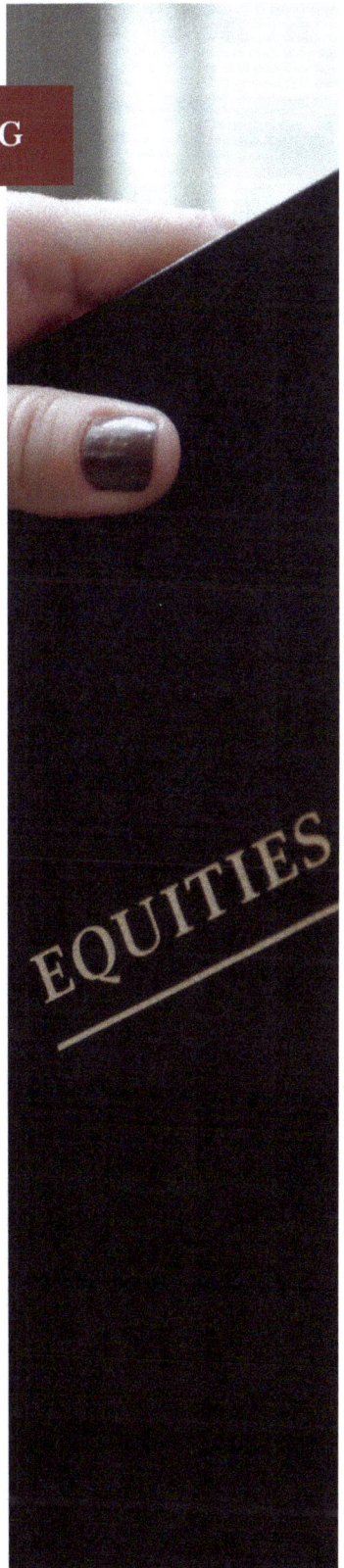

3.

"BONDS"

Bonds are a financial instrument that act as a loan from someone to a company, government or other entity such as certain agencies. Essentially, a company sells a bond to the public getting the proceeds from that sale in cash which can be used for the corporate purposes they decide.

In return, the purchasers of the bond gets a risky guarantee that they will receive back the money they lent to the company plus something to make it worthwhile. The money returned back is the Principal, the extra that makes the loan worthwhile is Interest.

Bonds carry varying rates of interest based on their risk, which is an assessment of the borrowing entity's ability to pay back the principal and make the interest payments.

4.

"OPTIONS & FUTURES"

Options and Futures are financial instruments that give the purchaser of the instruments some rights. The instruments are generally tied to stocks and other securities like commodities.

In the case of Futures, the purchaser is *obligated* to buy or sell some asset. In the case of Options, the purchaser *gets the option* to buy or sell some asset. This obligation or option is the major difference between them.

An example: One can buy a Futures contract to purchase the S&P 500 at a certain price on a certain date. A Futures contract is something that must occur. One can also buy an Options contract for the same asset, but here, the purchaser has the option to buy the S&P 500, not the obligation.

5.

"CALL OPTION"

A Call Option is a financial instrument that one can buy that allows the buyer the option to BUY an asset, most commonly, stocks. A Call Option gives one the option to buy a stock at a specific price on a given day. With stock, one option controls 100 shares.

An example. I believe the price of Apple stock which is now $100 will go to $200. To increase my financial success, I buy an option that allows me to get 100 shares of Apple at $100 dated 3 months from today. My hope in buying a Call Option on Apple at $100 is that its price is something higher in 3 months.

Options are risky, because if the stock doesn't go up in price sufficiently, the Call Option will expire worthless and all the investment will be lost.

6.

"PUT OPTION"

A Put Option is a financial instrument that one can buy that allows the buyer the option to SELL an asset, most commonly stocks. A Put Option gives one the option to sell a stock at a specific price on a given day. With stock, one option controls 100 shares.

An example. I believe the price of Apple stock which is now $200 will go to $100. To increase my possible profit, I buy an option that allows me to sell 100 shares of Apple at $200 three months from today. The hope is the price of Apple drops to $100, and now I have the option to sell it at $200.

Put Options are risky, because if the stock doesn't go down in price, the Put Option will expire worthless and all the investment will be lost.

7.

"TREASURY BILLS / NOTES / BONDS"

This category of debt instruments, Treasury Bills, Notes and Bonds are governmental bonds issued by a Federal government. They offer principal and interest payments and their repayments are guaranteed by the Federal government.

The only difference between Treasury Bills, Treasury Notes and Treasury Bonds is the time frame of the loan to the government. Treasury Bills are debt instruments of less than two years. Treasury Notes are debt instruments of between two and 10 years. Treasury Bonds are debt instruments of 10 years or greater. The longest Treasury Bond the US government issues is currently the 30 year bond. There is talk of a 50 year bond, but one has never been issued.

8.

"GOVERNMENT BONDS"

Government Bonds is a large category of bonds issued by a government, most usually the Federal government of a country. In essence, it is a loan to the government issuing the bond. These bonds most often offer an interest rate and will make principal and interest payments based on the amount of the bond held by the bondholder.

Government Bonds come in different forms based on time until expiration, the day when the issuer returns the principal. They come in a range of expiration dates from very short term (1 to 3 months) to very long term (30 years). The principal and interest of the bonds are guaranteed by what is known as "the full faith and credit" of the issuing institution, in this case, the federal government, which is guaranteeing repayment.

9.

"MONEY MARKET FUND"

A Money Market Fund is a type of mutual fund that invests specifically and solely in short-term assets, most often very short-term federal government and municipal bonds with an expiration of less than two years. It is a type of fund that is extremely riskless because of the nature of the holdings in the funds, that is short-term government bonds which are secured by the US government.

Many times the cash balance in investment accounts, and even cash balances in bank accounts, will be invested in Money Market Funds so that the cash balance generates some tangible financial return over time, interest, if not an overwhelmingly great one.

10.

"MORTGAGE BACKED SECURITIES"

Mortgage-Backed Securities (MBS) are a type of bond instrument that are made up of a large amalgam of underlying mortgages that have been grouped together and sold as one debt instrument. The bond elements themselves, by that I mean the payment of interest and repayment of principle to the bondholders, are backed by the mortgage payments of the underlying mortgages supporting the bond.

Mortgage-Backed Securities are more risky than government securities, as we found out during the Financial Crisis of 2007-09, because they are not backed by the US government, and mortgage defaults can skyrocket. However, on the whole over time, they have been a fine investment as a manageable percentage of one's investment holdings.

11.

"MUNICIPAL BONDS"

Municipal Bonds are government debt instruments issued by a municipal authority such as a state, city, township or even a municipal taxing authority, like a highway toll authority. Like other governmental bonds, Municipal Bonds pay interest and return principal with the payments backed by the revenues generated by the issuing authority.

While there are several different variations of Municipal Bonds, those supported on tax revenues, on toll revenues or a combination of both, it is important to note that Municipal Bonds, often referred to as Muni Bonds, are riskier than Federal government bonds, and in fact, some but extremely few have defaulted. However, it is equally important to note Muni Bonds are usually triple tax free, meaning the interest one receives is not taxed on any level, city, state or federal, which adds to their popularity.

Municipal Building

POLICE

12.

"EXCHANGE TRADED FUND (ETF)"

Now the most popular investment format, the Exchange Traded Fund (ETF) is a relatively recent invention in the investing world. An ETF represents a collection of stocks or other financial instruments tied together in one investible asset that trades on an exchange like a stock. There are almost endless different types of ETFs available for purchase.

All ETFs are in fact an index, a mathematical calculation, which is designed to represent a larger investment pool. The most common are based on things such as the S&P 500 and the NASDAQ 100. In practice, when one buys an ETF, one is buying a tiny portion of each stock in the index it is tied to. As a result, ETFs offer investors the benefits of a mutual fund in the format of a single stock.

13.

"EXCHANGE TRADED NOTES (ETN)"

An Exchange Traded Note (ETN) is an investible asset that trades like a bond, but represents a collection of other bond instruments. Similar in some regards to an ETF in its index nature, but in the case of the ETN, it acts more like a bond in that it repays principal at its termination. ETFs can be held indefinitely as they don't terminate.

Again similar to ETFs, Exchange Traded Notes come in a vast variety of options that are tied to different bond and equity indexs. However, different from ETFs, ETNs though they are often tied to bond instruments, do not pay periodic interest.

14.

"INDEX FUND"

An Index Fund is an ETF that is tied to a specific index, for example the Dow Jones Industrial Average. The ETF is designed to mimic the results of that index. An Index Fund can be linked to almost any financial index, both stock and bond Index Funds exist.

The largest, most popular Index Funds are the SPY ETF and the QQQ ETF which track the S&P500 stock index and the NASDAQ 100 stock index, respectively. In essence, by buying the Index Funds, one is buying a very small piece, perhaps infinitesimally small, of each stock in that index, essentially 500 companies in the first. Other ETFs track even larger indexes such as the Russell 2000 ETFs and the All World ETFs, which track global stock trading indexes.

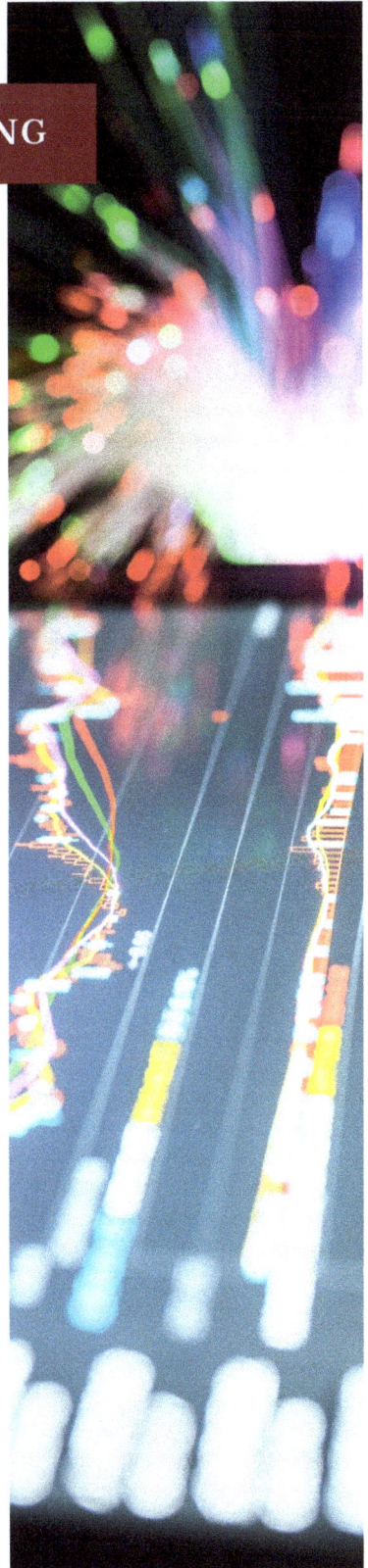

15.

"MUTUAL FUND"

A Mutual Fund is a pooled investment structure where investors purchase shares in a fund, which in turn, invests the money they receive in some financial asset, very often stocks, but not exclusively. Of course, the Mutual Fund receives fees for managing the investments, that's how it makes money.

Though substantially replaced by ETFs by more cost-conscious individual Investors over the last two decades, Mutual Funds remain a multi trillion dollar business, with various funds coming in an incredible variety of different types. Usually, they are tailored to the type of investments the fund purchases and specializes in, for example, Stock, Bond, mixture, etc. Mutual Funds are either Open-ended or Close-ended in their structure.

16.

"OPEN-ENDED FUNDS, CLOSED-ENDED FUND"

Generally, mutual funds can be categorized into two categories: Open-ended Funds or Closed Ended Funds. In theory, the main distinction between the two has to do with how a fund issues shares in its fund.

An Open-ended Fund issues new shares in the fund everytime someone buys shares in the fund. The buyer is buying, in essence, newly-created shares allowing for the purchase. All Closed-ended Funds sell shares only once at the inception/launch and do not sell new shares again. Hence it is closed to creating new shares. Both types of funds are available to buy and sell by the public, it's just the share-funding style that is the difference. For both, the value of the fund is tied to the Net Asset value (NAV) of the assets it owns.

17.

"SECURED/UNSECURED DEBT"

The debt a company has, ie., monies owed to either a person, business or institution, can be Secured or Unsecured. The difference between these two is whether some asset of the company has been pledged specifically against the money owed. This becomes very important if a company were to go bankrupt.

An example: A company has borrowed $20,000 from a bank and pledged a building purchased with the money against that loan. Now that loan (read: debt) is secured by the value of the building. If the company were to go bankrupt, the bank would have the right to sell the building to recoup the money on its loan.

Unsecured debt is not tied to any specific asset, and is much riskier as a result. The lender can only recoup money if there are leftover assets in the business.

18.

"HEDGE FUND"

A Hedge Fund is a pooled investment instrument that has the ability to invest for the owners of the pool in countless investing strategies, from both long and short positions (see definitions), and even more exotic approaches. The Hedge Fund is only limited by the bylaws of the fund, setup at its inception, which govern what can and cannot be invested in.

The name comes from its original use, which allowed the investment managers to hedge trading positions to lower overall risk through their approach. However, the name has become a broader umbrella to mean all types of private pooled investment vehicles. Often, but not always, access to Hedge Fund investment opportunities are limited to those investors with a proven level of investing experience and net worth.

19.

"LONG-ONLY & LONG-SHORT FUNDS"

Many Mutual funds are specifically designed in their bylaws that set up the fund, to be limited to the types of investments they can make. This is done to assure potential investors what the fund will invest in by limiting the fund manager's choice.

Long Only Funds are the most common type of limited funds by far. Here the Fund manager can only invest in stocks with a long position, that is purchasing stocks that they believe will increase in value. This differentiates these funds from what is known as Long-Short Funds, which have the freedom in their bylaws to also short stocks, that is sell them in advance hoping the stock price will drop (see other page for explanation).

20.

"AMERICAN DEPOSITORY RECEIPTS (ADR)"

American Depository Receipts are in essence foreign company stocks that are trading on an American stock exchange. They act exactly like any other normal stock, but since the company is a foreign domiciled company, the stock is designed as an ADR as opposed to a standard stock.

The ADR stock is issued through an American depository bank, and listed on an American exchange. This allows American investors to directly purchase shares of a foreign company without the impossible task of opening a bank account in a foreign country and purchasing the stock on that country's stock exchange or wherever that company is listed.

21.

"COMMODITIES"

A very broad category of assets sits under the headline, Commodities, but generally they are physical assets that are traded on exchanges similarly to stocks. Like the photo here shows, the wide ranging assets can run the gamut from gasoline to coffee to physical metals to even cattle like the famously known, Pork Belly prices.

Commodities as an investment help diversify a portfolio, and can act as an inflation hedge. For the average investor, unless you have very extensive knowledge in a specific commodity field and real experience in trading the asset-- which makes you not the average investor--one or more Commodities ETFs is the best investment alternative for this asset class.

22.

"PRECIOUS METALS, NON-PRECIOUS METALS"

Two categories within the larger category of commodities is Precious Metals and Non-Precious metals. Given their nature, the average price between the two can vary greatly. One metal is generally considered Precious because of its relative rarity on earth.

Precious Metals that are traded specifically are Gold, Silver, Palladium, Platinum. Some other more obscure metals are traded as well. These Precious Metals have been designated of particular value for many centuries dating back thousands of years. Common examples of Non-Precious Metals are Copper, Brass, Aluminum, Steel etc. Their abundance on Earth affects their availability, and as a result their deemed value in the marketplace.

23.

"MÊME STOCKS"

A relatively new phrase in the world of investing, Même Stocks are stocks that a certain portion of the stock investing world is pushing through social media. These stocks become famous, or perhaps infamous is better, because of this social media push into the spotlight. As a result, these stocks sometimes undergo meteoric rises and crushing falls, oftentimes in a very short period of time, and even possibly in the same day.

Investing in a Même Stock is not for the faint of heart as it often more resembles gambling than it does investing. The movements from day to day can be rather extreme, often not based on sound, solid financial information or analysis. They are not recommended for long-term investors.

24.

"DIVIDENDS"

Most simply, Dividends are payments made by a company to the shareholders of that company. Dividends are made from the excess cash the company has in reserve, and usually are only paid when the reserves are so sufficient that the company cannot effectively use the excess cash to grow the business.

Many fast-growing companies, like technology companies, do not pay a Dividend as the company has what it believes are excellent projects to invest their cash in, projects that will fund future growth. However, oftentimes, older companies in slower growing industries, like banks or industrial companies, don't have enough growth projects to invest in so they return the excess cash the business generates. Dividends can be paid monthly, quarterly or annually. A company is not obligated to pay dividends.

25.

"STOCK SPLIT"

From time to time, a public company, one trading on a stock exchange, will decide to do a Stock Split, essentially cutting their stock price while giving current shareholders more shares to compensate for the cutting of their stock price. In the end, after the cutting of price and suppling shares, the shareholder is in exactly the same position of value as before these moves. Thus, Stock Splits do NOT create any value for the shareholders.

However, many times, stocks do rise in value in response to the announcement of a Stock Split. Generally it is believed that the lowering of the stock price increases the number of potential investors in a stock, since the market size has grown and this drives interest in the stock. This is generally tied to companies with a stock price that is extremely high.

26.

"THE FEDERAL RESERVE BANK AND SYSTEM"

The Federal Reserve Bank and its system of subordinate Banks beneath it, act as the bank of the United States of America without technically being the bank of the United States. It handles the banking functions for the Federal government and sets short-term interest rate policies as an act of its role in setting what is known as Monetary policy, which it controls to a certain tangible degree.

The Federal Reserve Bank and its system of banks support and regulate the larger banking system of which almost all public and private banks are a part. "The Fed" as it is known, has two goals mandated by Congress: One is maximizing employment, and the other is price stability.

27.

"TO BE LONG SOMETHING"

To Be Long something, most typically stocks, is when we have ownership of that something through a purchase of it. We have purchased 100 shares of Apple stock so we are long Apple stock.

Most generally, we "go" Long something when we believe it is going to go up in value. So in the case where we buy Apple shares, we did this because we believe that Apple shares are going to go up in value. That is, we "went" long Apple shares because we believe the shares will appreciate.

The vast majority of investors own shares in a company, thus are Long, because they believe the stock of the company is going to go up.

28.

"TO BE SHORT SOMETHING"

In Finance, when we say that we are short something, it means that we believe that something is going down in value, usually stocks, and we have taken steps to create profits from this belief.

Generally with stocks, when we "go" short a stock, we borrow stock from someone else to sell them, normally a major brokerage investment company, knowing we have to return this stock at a later date. The hope is that the stock drops in value so that we can purchase the stock at a lower price than we borrowed it at, return it, thus making a profit.

Going Short is quite risky as something can rise in price unlimitedly, and we'll have to replenish the borrowed stock at higher price even infinitely high.

29.

"BULLS AND BEARS"

Bulls and Bears are nicknames for someone's position on where they think the price of an asset is heading. If someone believes that the price of an asset is going to go up, that person is a Bull on that something. If someone believes that the price of an asset is going to go down, that person is a Bear on that asset.

We often also use the adjectives Bullish and Bearish to describe the person who has an opinion on the future price of an asset.

An easy way to remember the meaning of the two words is to think of how each animal attacks. A Bull rears upward when it attacks and a Bear attacks downward when it attacks.

30.

"BULL & BEAR MARKET"

Though no hard and fast law exists defining what is a Bull Market or a Bear Market, for most followers of the stock market, a 20% price movement is where a Bull or Bear Market begins. This has been the standard definition for eons.

To explain in detail, when a stock market has proceeded in a specific direction for a period time, let's say downward, it eventually reaches its lowest point. When the stock market goes up more than 20% from that recent lowest point, it is said to have entered a Bull Market. Likewise but conversely, when the market drops 20% from a recent high point, it is said to have entered a Bear Market. This can apply also to individual stocks as well, with their corresponding 20% movements in either direction being defined as entering Bull or Bear Market territory.

31.

"MARKET CORRECTION"

A Market Correction is when a stock market has fallen at least 10% from a recent high level. To be even more precise, a Correction is when the stock market has fallen between 10% and 20% exactly, because a fall of greater than 20% is referred to as a Bear Market.

Stock Market Corrections are not uncommon events, they often happen a couple times a year, and can even occur during Bull Market period. Hence a correction is not really the destruction that a Bear Market is.

It is important to note that the use of the word, Correction, meaning the 10% downward rule can also apply to individual stocks when they too fall between 10 and 20% from a recent high level. In that case, it would be said that a stock has corrected.

32.

"NET ASSET VALUE (NAV)"

Net Asset Value (NAV) is a financial calculation and the common metric by which most Mutual Funds are valued. It is a measurement of the size of the fund and its worth as it calculates the total assets that a fund has minus the liabilities that reduce the value of the assets in the fund.

NAV is often a useful tool for comparing mutual funds based on size which can be important to some investors. Generally, but not always, the size of the fund suggests that length of time the fund has been in operation, and it can also be an implication of market confidence in the fund managers as a large fund has more money to invest. Larger NAVs do not mean greater returns, in fact sometimes large funds inhibit greater returns.

91

33.

"MARKET VALUE / MARKET CAPITALIZATION"

Market Value, and Market Capitalization are synonyms, they represent the total value of a company as defined in the marketplace. This is defined by the stock market, and not in an accounting sense. It is derived by multiplying the price per share at a given point in time against the total number of shares outstanding.

An example: Company XYZ has a total of 1,000,000 shares outstanding. Its share price, the cost for one share of stock, is $10 at the end of day on a stock market. So the market value/capitalization of the company is $10 Million, shares times share price.

34.

"EARNINGS PER SHARE"

A core measure of a company, its success or failings, Earnings Per Share is a simple calculation and one that is a part of almost every smart investment discussion. It is a metric that allows us to compare a company's history against itself, and in some instances, to compare various stocks against each other.

Simply, one divides the earnings of a company in total by the total number of shares outstanding in the marketplace. As an example, if a company earns $1 Millon in profit, and it has in total 10 million shares outstanding, the Earnings Per Share is 10¢. The Earnings Per Share is normally calculated on either a quarterly or annual basis for comparison.

35.

"REALIZED / UNREALIZED GAINS (PROFITS)"

In business, generally, we do not pay taxes on profits that have not been Realized yet. What this means is, we only pay taxes on profits that have been generated because we bought then actually sold the asset, there by creating a Realized Gain. It is the act of selling the asset and generating a profit that makes it "realized."

If we have a profit on an asset, but we have not yet sold the asset, we say that the profit is Unrealized. Unrealized profits are not taxable because we cannot know the future and we don't know if the Unrealized gains will remain in existence in the future. By selling the asset and realizing the profit, we know the profit exists and thus taxes must be paid.

36.

"DURATION"

Duration is a measurement of the weighted average time that cash flows are received from some asset. Various assets pay different cash flows to the owner of the asset. These cash flows often are received in different periods. Duration measures, as a weighted average, how long all the cashflows are received.

An example: I buy a bond that comes due in 5 years from today. The cash flows that I'll receive will be interest for five years then I will receive back the principal on the bond. Duration will measure the weighted average in years of the cashflows coming to me. $500 in interest each year, then $5,000 returned in the end.

In general, an investor wants to shorten their duration when interest rates are rising, and lengthen their duration when interest rates are falling.

37.

"BID / ASK
BID-ASK RATIO"

A stock market is just that, a market for stocks, similar to any market for goods. There is someone wanting sell at a price, and someone who wants to buy at a price. A stock exchange brings those people together to hopefully find a deal between them.

A Bid is the price offer to buy made by the potential buyer. An Ask is a price offer to sell made by the potential seller. The Bid-Ask Ratio calculates the number of buyers making Bids versus the number of Sellers making Asks. When there are higher Bids it shows overall interest in stock, and conversely when there are higher Asks, it shows overall interest in selling.

38.

"MARKET ORDER"

When placing an order to buy an amount of shares of stock trading on a stock exchange, there are various types of orders one can place, and the most common is a Market Order. A Market Order is when the order will be completed at whatever price the stock is trading at the precise moment the order is placed.

As an example, if one wants to purchase 1 share of Apple stock, and it is a Market Order, that order will be executed at whatever the current price for Apple shares are trading when the order is communicated to the market and executed. It is not an order at a specific set price, but merely an order executed at whatever price the stock is trading at currently.

39.

"LIMIT ORDER"

In contrast to a Market Order, a Limit Order is when a stock order is placed with a broker at a specific price exactly (the Limit Price). This contrasts with a Market Order which takes whatever price is available in the market at the time of placing the order.

In the instance of a Limit Order, the client will communicate the exact price they are willing to pay or sell a stock, usually with the amount of shares they want in total. For example, if you wanted to buy 10 shares of Apple at exactly $85.35, this would be communicated to the broker, and the purchase of shares would not occur at any price higher than that exact price. If the price of Apple remains above the Limit price, the purchase will never be executed.

40.

"STOP LOSS ORDER"

A Stop Loss order is essentially a Limit order placed by someone who wants to limit their downside risk, that is, the falling of a stock price. The goal is to protect oneself from losing too much money on any stock purchases.

It works as follows: You buy a stock, and just after, you place a Stop Loss order with your broker for a specific price. You choose the price, and if that price is matched in the marketplace, your stock is sold automatically at the market without any effort on your part. Many stock investors will set a Stop Loss order on a consistent metric across their stock holdings, for example a 20% reduction from the purchase price.

41.

"GOOD TILL CANCELLED ORDER"

A related element of a Limit Order for stocks, Good Till Cancelled is a choice a purchaser or seller can make when placing a Limit order with a broker. In essence, it tells the broker to keep the request to purchase/buy at a specific given price open for longer than the current day of trading in which the order was communicated.

For example, if a person places a Limit order with a broker for 10 shares of Apple at $85.35, it can place that order with the caveat of Good Till Cancelled. This choice will keep this Limit order open for an extended period beyond, and sometimes far beyond, the given day that the purchase request was made. In the future, if the Limit price is reached, the order will be executed provided it is during the Good Till Cancelled period, which can be long, but is not unlimited.

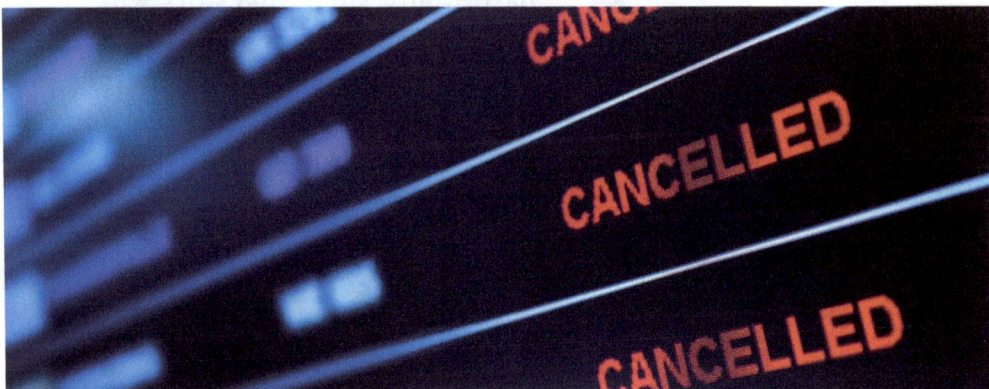

42.

"PENNY STOCKS"

The name is a bit of an anachronism now that pennies are no longer being printed, but Penny Stocks still exist and still trade on major stock exchanges.

Penny stocks are the stocks of publicly traded companies that trade on major exchanges that are usually priced under $2 and often priced less than $1.

While these companies do exist and their shares are traded on exchanges an investor needs to remain very careful when choosing to invest in these stocks. There is a reason why the company is trading at such a low price, and it is usually not a good reason (lack of revenue or profitability). Additionally, the stocks can have huge swings in either direction without warning because of their low price, and this can lead to sometimes great profits and sometimes great losses.

43.

"REAL ESTATE INVESTMENT TRUSTS (REITS)"

Real Estate Investment Trusts, abbreviated in financial circles as REITs, are a legal structure company that invest in real estate properties that produce income through rents. They may own apartment buildings or malls or cell phone towers. These properties are packaged together in the legal entity that makes up the REIT.

Some REITs are publicly traded companies that are traded on the stock exchange. Investors like investing in REITs because they have a steady consistent cash flow, and as a result of this, pay good dividends, and sometimes exceptionally high dividends. As always, there are risks involved, an investors need to be careful.

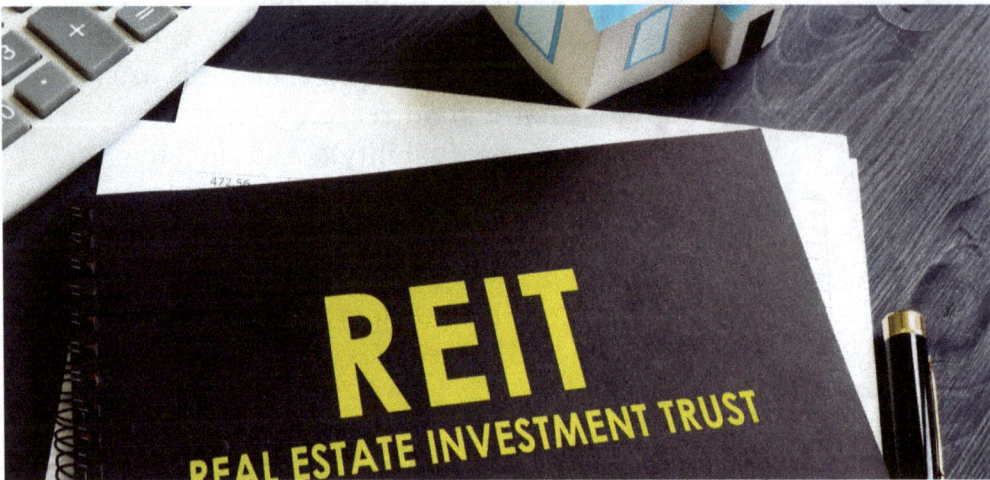

44.

"30 DAY SEC YIELD"

Differing from the common calculation of investments yield which are on an annual basis, the 30-Day SEC Yield is related to the income produced by the asset over the last 30 days. Giving it shorter time frame it gives a different take on what the current yield of the asset is during its recent period.

If interest rates have moved considerably over a short period of time, let's say because the Federal Reserve has made substantial policy changes, the 30-day SEC you may be a better indicator than the traditional yield calculation as it factors in more recent income generation based on higher or lower recent rates. The 30-day SEC yield is usually shown next to the traditional yield calculation for comparison.

45.

"LISTING / DELISTING"

Listing is when a publicly traded company begins trading on a financial stock exchange like the New York Stock Exchange (NYSE) or the NASDAQ. It's called 'Listing' as the company's ticker symbol is listed with all the other companies available for sale on the exchange.

Delisting is the removal of a publicly-traded stock from trading on a stock exchange. It can happen for several reasons such as a under $1 stock price, which exchanges don't accept, or the company has been sold and is no longer public. For whatever reason the stock is removed from trading on the exchange eliminating the possibility of buying or selling it.

46.

"SHORT VS LONG TERM CAPITAL GAINS"

It is important to note that the United States, and many other countries around the world, tax capital gains quite differently depending on how long an investor has owned the asset, more specifically, usually stocks. The difference between Short-Term Capital Gains and Long-Term Capital Gain tax rates can be substantial, and often do and should affect one's investment decisions.

Currently in the US, the difference is between 10% for long term gains (those held over 1 year) and a minimum of 30%+ short term gains (held under 1 year). It is important to note that capital gains tax laws are subject to change by the government at any time, potentially either increasing or decreasing.

47.

"STOCK CANDLES"

Stock Candles represent the movement of a stock during a specific time period, which can be 1 minute, 5 minutes, an hour, a month, a year, any period. It is made up of two elements, the lines at the top and bottom of the box which are called Wicks, and the Body of the candle, most often rectangular shape, which typically are red for down and green for up.

When a candle box is green that means during this period the lower end of the rectangular box represents where the stock opened during the time period and the top of the box represents where it closed during the time period. It is the opposite for a red candle, the bottom of the box is where it closed and the top of the box is where it opened. The Wicks represent movement made during the time, but not a closure.

48.

"COVERED / NAKED CALLS"

Covered Calls are a particular situation where an investor has written a call, which gives another party the right to purchase a stock at a specific price on a specific day, when they already own the shares to back up the call they've written in their investment account. The writer of the call receives a fee from the buyer of the call in order to incent them to create the call.

A Naked Call is a situation where an investor has written a call option, but in this instance, they do not already own the shares to cover the call in their investment account. This can be extremely risky if the market moves in unexpected ways and many types of investment accounts do not allow it.

49.

"REVERSE SPLIT"

When a stock price drops below $1, it risks the stock exchange it trades on delisting it and no longer allowing it to be traded on the exchange. Obviously this event is extremely harmful to the company. Often companies with even a very low price will do a Reverse Split to get the price higher.

To overcome this predicament many companies will do what is known as a Reverse Split, which acts in a manner opposite to a normal stock split. Here the number of shares outstanding of the company are cut in half and the stock price is doubled. The company with 5 million shares outstanding will reduce its float to 2.5 million shares, and their stock price will adjust from $2.50 to $5.

50.

"TRACKING STOCKS"

For a couple reasons that exist, Tracking Stocks are a stock that has been floated on the market with the purpose of moving in exact sync with another basis stock or index. In essence, it "tracks" exactly what another stock or index does, meaning the basis stock's movement up or down.

The Tracking Stock merely is a different, more accessible form of the basis stock. Example: The true cost of a Berkshire Hathaway A stock is currently over $750,000 for one share (yes, you read that right). A tracking stock was released to the market that moves in lockstep with the core basis Berkshire Hathaway stock. Its current price is just over $500. This tracking stock moves in lockstep with the core stock

INVESTING BASICS

INVESTMENT ANALYSIS

ESSENTIAL INVESTING BASICS

51.

"PRICE EARNINGS RATIO (P.E. RATIO)"

One of the most important Investments metrics in investment analysis is the Price Earnings Ratio often abbreviated to the PE ratio or just even the PE. It is a metric that relates the price of a company's stock on a stock market to the amount of earnings per share that the company has or is expecting to earn.

As an example to calculate, imagine a company earns $3 per share of stock outstanding and the company's stock is currently trading at $100. By dividing $100 by $3, we get a P.E. of 33.3. Thus this company is trading at 33 times its earning per share. The PE Ratio changes constantly as the stock price changes moment to moment on an exchange. Additionally, as companies' earnings change or the forecast for them change, this also will change the PE ratio.

52.

"P.E.G. RATIO"

A more advanced version of the PE Ratio is the Price Earnings Growth ratio, otherwise known as the PEG ratio. This ratio relates the PE Ratio of the company with the projected earnings growth of that company.

Let's take an example: A company has a PE Ratio of 20, which means a company is trading at 20 times its earnings per share. If the company is expected to grow its earnings at 40% per year, it has a PEG Ratio of 2. The earnings growth divided by the PE Ratio.

Generally, investors like to invest in companies with a higher PEG ratio, as in some ways, it represents a good value relative to other companies with a lower PEG Ratio.

53.

"TRAILING TWELVE MONTHS EARNINGS (TTM)"

In investing, there are two ways of looking at a company's earning: One of them is known as the Trailing Twelve Months earnings, often abbreviated as TTM on reports, and the other is Forward Earnings.

The Trailing Twelve Months earnings figure calculates the total earnings per share that a company has generated over the last twelve months, not the last calendar year. This figure is often used in the calculation of the PE Ratio of a company, which is the company's stock price divided by these Trailing Twelve Months earnings per share.

54.

"FORWARD P/E RATIO"

As compared to the trailing twelve months version of this analysis, the Forward P/E Ratio (see photo below), calculates the metric based on using the Forward-Looking estimate for earnings as opposed to using the actually-occurred past twelve months earnings achieved.

More often than not, the Forward PE Ratio is smaller than the Trailing Twelve months version because companies are expected to increase their earnings in the coming year. This represents the benefit of growing earnings in the value of a stock price. However, if future earnings are expected to slow down in coming years, the Forward PE Ratio will be higher than the Trailing Twelve Months version. Not a great sign.

55.

"FUNDAMENTAL ANALYSIS"

One of the two main Financial Analysis approaches used to forecast individual stocks, stock markets and other tradable assets, is Fundamental Analysis. This is the traditional approach most put forward by financial analysts on Wall Street.

Fundamental Analysis is in essence analyzing assets based on "the fundamentals" underlying each asset. For stocks, it is most often Revenue, Cash Flow and Profit growth, etc. Traditional metrics, that is. Fundamental Analysis is often used as a tool to compare different stocks and assets against each other to help foresee upcoming pricing trends.

When done most effectively, Fundamental Analysis leads to better investing decisions.

56.

"TECHNICAL ANALYSIS"

One of the two main Financial Analysis approaches used to forecast individual stocks, stock markets and other tradable assets is Technical Analysis. It is a less traditional, quite a bit more obscure approach to forecasting and predicting asset price movements. It is based on the theory that moves in asset prices will follow recurring and recognizable patterns over time.

Its main belief is that by studying those past patterns and studying current movements in asset prices will offer insight and clues to the next movements. While sometimes this approach seems farfetched, even counterintuitive, it is essential to recognize that many investors follow this approach and that it affects markets as a result.

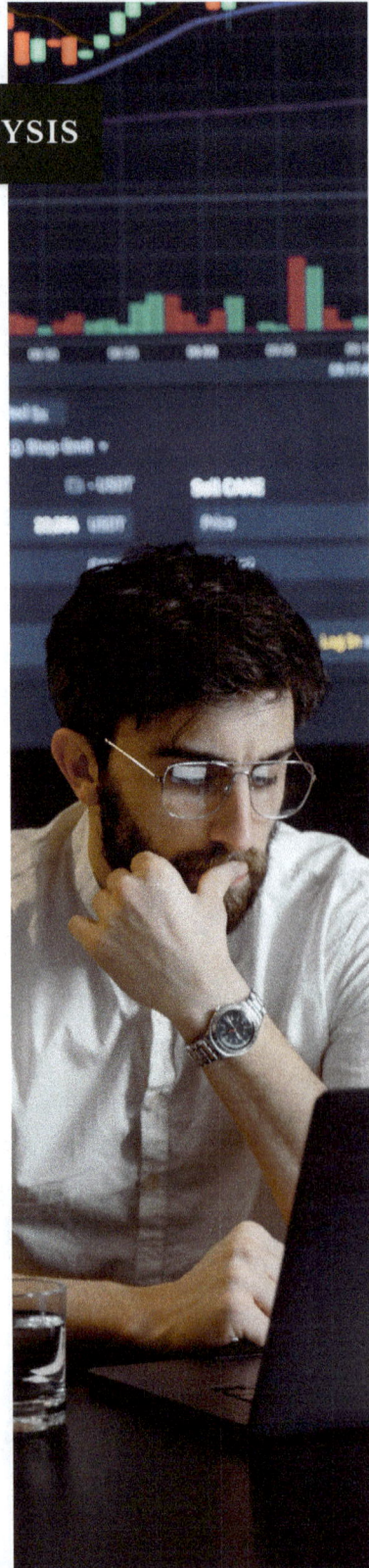

57.

"GROWTH STOCKS"

Very broadly speaking, investors often talk of stocks falling into one of two categories: Growth Stocks and Value Stocks. The main difference between the two is in the rate of growth in their earnings from year to year. However, sometimes the line is blurry.

Growth Stocks are, as the name implies, those stocks that are growing their earnings at a great rate from year to year. To be considered a Growth Stock, the earnings should be growing generally in excess of 10% per year, often much more than that.

A lot of technology companies tend to fall in this category. We can often think of Facebook or Google or Amazon, which have achieved tremendous year-over-year earnings growth over a substantial, sustained period of time.

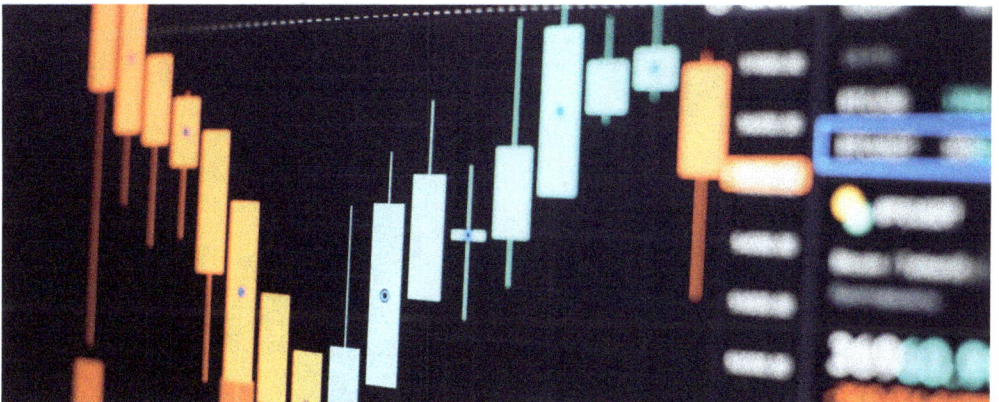

58.

"VALUE STOCKS"

Very broadly speaking, investors often talk of stocks falling into one of two categories: Growth Stocks and Value Stocks. The main difference between the two is in the rate of growth in their earnings from year to year.

Value Stocks are those stocks who earnings are growing at a slow rate from year to year, and sometimes barely at all. They are called Value Stocks because they trade at a low multiple of earnings, and can offer great value because of this low PE multiple.

This category of stocks is characterized by many old-line industries such as banks, heavy equipment companies and utilities. That is, companies whose high growth days are mostly behind them. They often pay a nice dividend to compensate investors for the slow growth of earnings.

59.

"FED FUNDS RATE"

The Federal Funds Rate, also known as the Fed Funds Rate, is the interest rate that the Federal Reserve Bank of the United States (The Fed) charges its member banks for loans the banks take from the Federal Reserve. Member Banks are the largest Global banks in the world with operations in the United States.

The Federal Reserve sets the Fed Funds Rate, and this rate acts in some manner, as a basis for most other interest rates that exist. The Fed uses the Fed Funds Rate to attempt to affect the United States economy, in theory slowing the economy by raising the rate, or conversely, lowering the rate in an attempt to grow the economy. As the Fed changes the rate, more or less loans are made at higher or lower interest rates, and thus business activities are affected.

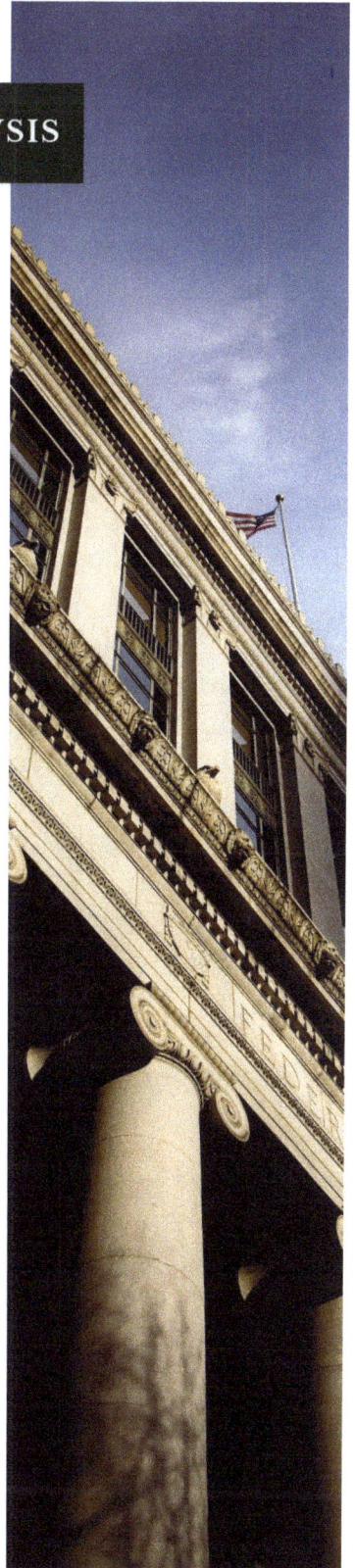

60.

"ASSETS UNDER MANAGEMENT (AUM)"

Assets Under Management, abbreviated as AUM, is a common term by which to measure the size in dollars of various financial funds or money management firms. It is a calculation of all the assets in dollar terms that are being managed by whichever entity it is describing. The assets can include all financial instruments such as stocks, bonds, cash, real estate, commodities, cryptocurrency etc.

Many companies or Financial Management entities will use Assets Under Management as a marketing tool to express their impressive size hoping to communicate a sense of acceptance and institutional support. Though AUM does connote size, it doesn't necessarily correspond with success.

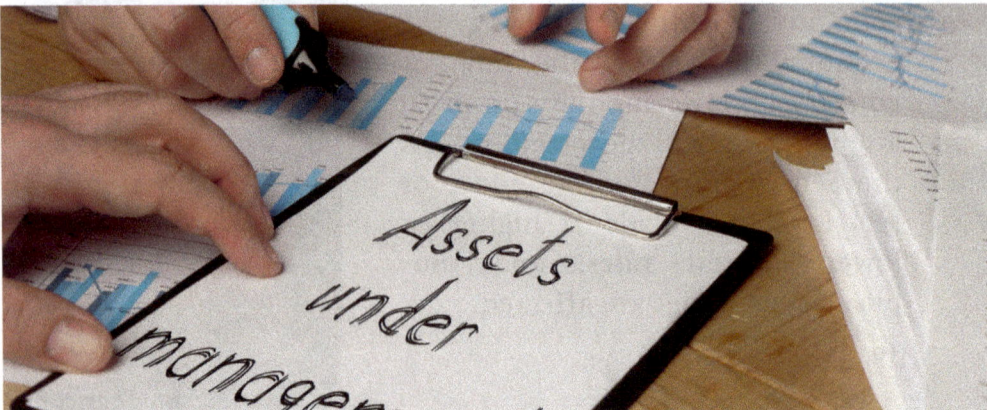

61.

"MONETARY POLICY"

As opposed to tax-and-spend influenced Fiscal Policy, Monetary Policy is the name given to the actions taken by the Federal Reserve Bank. The Federal Reserve sets Monetary Policy through adjustments to various banking lending elements, most prominently the Federal Funds Rate. This interest rate, again set by the The Federal Reserve Bank, is the rate charged to the country's very largest banks for very short term loans.

The Federal Reserve (The Fed) adjusts elements it controls in order to try to affect the country's economy. We give the name Monetary Policy to these efforts the Fed takes to adjust the economy, be it raising or dropping interest rates and adjusting other bank requirements such loan reserves.

62.

"FISCAL POLICY"

Broadly speaking, Fiscal Policy refers to the policies by the Federal government, excluding those of the Federal Reserve bank, to affect the economy. This includes tax policies and spending policies which are implemented through either legally-passed budgets or laws which design, determine and implement spending programs.

Each presidential administration enacts its Fiscal Policy as it seems fit, though it is often limited in the actions it can take because of legal statutes and sometimes the efforts of the other party, if they control one or more houses of Congress. However, by adjusting taxing and spending policies, an administration can substantially affect the economy of the country via this, its Fiscal Policy.

63.

"THE FED'S DUAL MANDATE"

The Dual Mandate refers to the goals set by Congress for the Federal Reserve in the founding legislation, The Federal Reserve Reform Act of 1977. The two goals are, in no particular order, Price Stability and Maximum Employment. They are equally important in the statute, neither more important than the other. Please note that neither are absolutes, neither total Price Stability nor total and complete Employment.

In fact, the two elements of the Fed's Dual Mandate are sometimes in conflict as moments occur when maximum employment can lead to price instability and vice versa. So the Dual Mandate is a balancing act that the Federal Reserve is charged with achieving.

64.

"YIELD / YIELDING"

Yield is term used in finance to refer to the return one can expect to earn on an investment. It is more often, but not solely, used with bond and other interest related investments, and represents the nominal interest rate associated with an investment.

For example, when one looks at purchasing a government bond, one should and will analyze to see what the bond is "yielding", that is, the amount of interest the bond will be paying to the bondholder (owner). If the bond is paying 5%, it is said that the bond is yielding 5%, meaning the bondholder will receive interest in the amount of 5% of the principal owned by the bondholder.

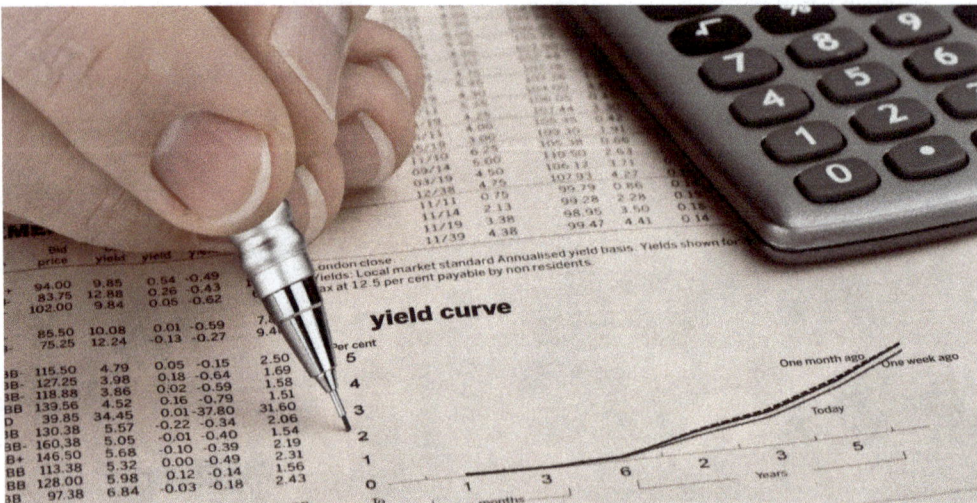

64.

"REAL VS. NOMINAL INTEREST RATE."

In Finance, it is important to understand the difference between the Real Interest Rate and the Nominal Interest Rate as this can affect investment decisions. Both rates are important to know as a result.

The Nominal Interest Rate is the "stated" interest rate. For instance, if the rate on a bought corporate bond is 5%, that's the nominal rate. The Real Interest Rate is the Nominal Interest Rate minus the current Inflation rate. If the Nominal Rate is 5%, and the inflation rate is 3%, the Real Interest Rate is 2%. In reality, the Real Interest Rate better reflects the true yield on an interest bearing security as it takes into account the effect of inflation, which lowers future purchasing power.

66.

"DIVIDEND YIELD"

The Dividend Yield is the percentage of money that a shareholder receives for owning a share of a company that pays a dividend (many do not pay a dividend). It is calculated by dividing the dividend the company declares for payment to shareholders (at their discretion) by the stock's current share price.

Let's say a company pays a dividend of $1 per share of stock and the current stock price is $50 on some publicly traded stock exchange. The Dividend Yield calculation would produce a dividend yield of 2% ($1 ÷ $50). It's important to know that each time the price of the company's stock changes, the Dividend Yield changes, if only slightly. But over long periods, dividend yields can change due to changes in the stock price or the declared dividend.

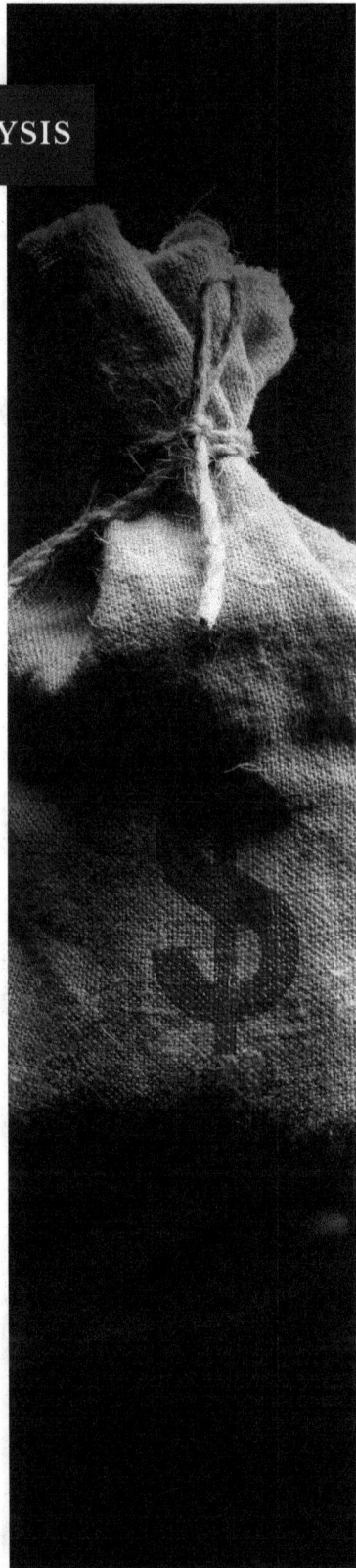

67.

"DIVIDEND AMOUNT"

When investors talk about dividends they will describe it in one of two ways, the Dividend Amount or the Dividend Yield. As described previously, the dividend yield is a calculation of the dividend payment relative to the stock price.

The Dividend Amount is the actual payment in dollar terms that the Investor will receive. The amount can be described either in quarterly or annual amounts, depending on the time frame the payment is made. It is normally stated on a per share basis, for example 30¢ per share, $1.50 per share, etc., depending on the timeframe and what the company declares publicly.

68.

"EX DIVIDEND DATE"

When a company declares publicly its period dividend (normally quarterly but not always), they will announce the amount per share they pay, but also they will announce the Ex Dividend Date. This is date for which the one must be a registered shareholder of the stock in order to receive the dividend payment when it occurs. The Ex Dividend Date is not the date when payments are made to shareholders.

As an example, Apple declares a dividend that goes Ex Dividend on June 30th. All shareholders that own the stock will receive the dividend payment when it is made regardless of whether they sell the shares they own after this date. If you don't own the shares before this date, you will not receive the dividend payment even if you buy shares the next day.

VESTME

69.

"THE YIELD CURVE."

The Yield Curve is a graphical representation that shows the adjusting relationship between different investing time lengths and interest rates. It is a crucial element to understand to invest in the bond market effectively.

Let's take the example of government bonds. Normally, the longer the bond (that is, the longer the period before principal is returned to the bondholder), the greater the interest rate on that bond. This accounts for the risks associated with longer periods of time. So the Yield Curve tracks graphically the difference between all different times to maturity, from very short (2 months - 3 years) to very long (7 years - 30 years). The Yield Curve is normally upward sloping for as time to maturity lengthens, generally the interest rate rises. But not always.

70.

"INVERTED YIELD CURVE."

In quite rare occasions, and often but not always proceeding a recession, there is a Yield Curve Inversion or an Inverted Yield Curve. This is often a sign of a disordered market, and a foreboding one.

An Inverted Yield Curve exists when short-term bonds are paying a greater interest rate than longer-term bonds. The usual relation of "higher interest rates with the longer the maturity" is upended by market forces. In these rare instances, for example, a bond with a 2-year maturity could be paying 5% interest where a bond with a 30-Year maturity could only be paying 4% interest. It happens because of unusual supply and demands elements in investor choices has created imbalances. Generally, it's not a good sign for the stock market or the economy.

130

71.

"STEEPENING YIELD CURVE"

A Steeping Yield Curve occurs when either short-term rates are dropping or long term rates are increasing or both are occuring at the same time. This phenomenon often occurs when the Federal Reserve Bank begins lowering the short term interest rate that it controls (the Fed Funds Rate).

When short-term interest rates are being lowered, investors usually look to lock in their investments in longer term bonds as these instruments will be paying higher rates of interest, and are less susceptible to price declines. A Steepening Yield Curve is normally a good sign after a period of a shallow or inverted yield curve as under normal circumstances, one is rewarded more for investing longer term. But there are limits to how steep is good.

72.

"INTEREST RATE CYCLES" TIGHTEN/LOOSEN

The Federal Reserve controls the Fed Funds Rate, which acts as the basis for which all other interest rates adjust by. Traditionally changes to this rate happen in a series of same-direction moves called an Interest Rate Cycle. The Cycle can be in either direction, both up and down. The cycles are driven by how the economy is doing.

A Tightening Cycle is a series of increases in the Fed Funds Rate. It is undertaken to slow down and overheating economy or one that is expected to overheat in the future. A Loosening Cycle is a series of decreases in the Fed Funds Rate and is undertaken to aid an economy that is slowing down or failing.

72.

"PAR"

The term Par is an essential concept in understanding bonds, bond investing and bond pricing especially. It is the basis for which the pricing of all new bonds are sold to the public, and the how they are valued on going.

When a bond is sold by an entity, be it a government, agency or company, it is sold at Par. This is the face value of the bond. It's generally represented by the number 100. After it is sold initially, and begins trading in the public markets, the price of the bond will adjust based on market forces, above or below 100, which remains par. The price represents the new value. When the bond is in demand, it will trade above Par (for example at 107.50 and when it is not in demand it will trade below par (.93).

74.

"BUY, HOLD, SELL RATINGS "

On Wall Street, there are many financial research firms that offer financial opinions on the price of financial assets, and in particular, on publicly traded stocks. Very often but not absolutely, firms will express their opinions on where a stock's price will go with different ratings in the form of Buy, Sell or Hold.

As one can expect, the guidance follows the wording with Buy and Sell being instructions to investors and Hold meaning to keep your position as is currently. Other houses will also Underperform, Market Perform, and Overperform as tiers of recommendation in place of Buy, Hold, Sell. In essence, different words but same meanings.

75.

"52 WEEK HIGH / LOW"

Two most-often watched metrics are the 52 Week High and Low. Easily enough, these are the extreme numbers that a given stock price has hit during a day in the last 52 weeks in terms of its highest or lowest number.

Many investors track the distance between the current price of a stock or index and one or both of these numbers. For example, people will rightly concern themselves if a stock is just 2% from its 52 Week High or say it is just 5% from a 52 Week Low. The proximity to the extreme numbers often give investors an idea as to when or when not to purchase a stock they are following.

Please note there is a difference between the 52 week numbers and all-time numbers (high or low), which are often different.

76.

"PRE-MARKET / AFTER MARKET TRADING"

Normal trading hours for the American Stock Exchanges are between 9:30 a.m. and 4 pm East Coast time. However, there are opportunities to trade outside of the normal trading hours for those willing to pay for the capacity and with the appropriate investment account settings.

Pre-Market Trading occurs before the market in the morning and can start as early as 4am EST. After Market Trading occurs after the market closes at 4pm and goes until 6:30pm. Compared to normal business hours, the volume traded during these times is very small and generally only completed by professional investment managers and traders. With small trading volumes often comes big swings.

77.

"PRODUCTIVE VS. NON-PRODUCTIVE ASSETS"

In certain Financial investing circles, a distinction is made between Productive Assets versus Non Productive Assets. Productive Assets are assets like stocks in businesses, real estate, even cash as they will create value over time through producing something.

Non-Productive Assets are those assets whose value is based on scarcity and limitations, and do not increase through a capacity to create value through its own productivity. Gold and other precious metals are the most well-known Non-Productive Asset.

A famous quote from the renowned investor and Warren Buffett partner, Charlie Munger, says that, "Gentleman do not invest in Non-Productive assets."

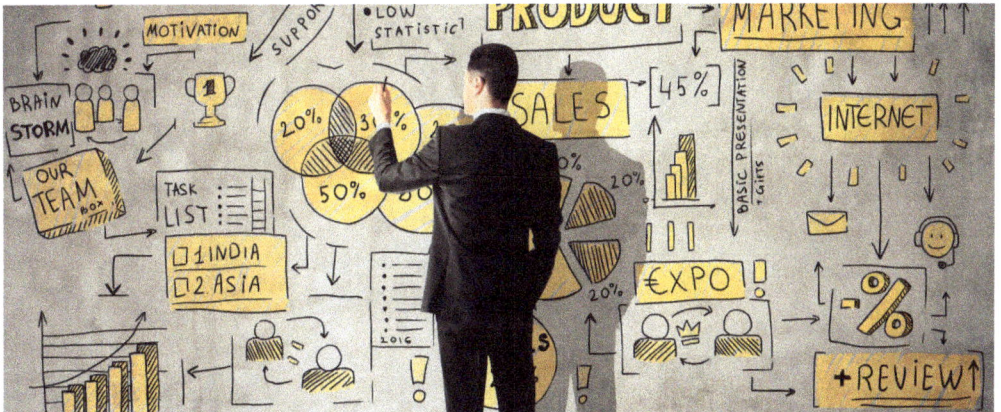

78.

"SHARE VOLUME"

Share Volume is a financial metric which tracks how many shares of a given stock or other publicly traded instrument are traded in a given day. The number is also calculated for the whole stock exchange market, for example the New York Stock Exchange, which represents the Share Volume for all shares exchanging hands of all stocks on the exchange.

Share Volume is often considered a metric which communicates both interest in a stock as well as knowledge of and acceptance of a stock. Stocks with high daily Share Volume are usually more well-known, more established, and have more interest in the minds of investors on a given day. The largest companies generally have the largest Share Volume.

79.

"UP / DOWN VOLUME"

In stock market investing, Volume is the amount of total shares traded in a period, usually calculated by the day. Volume can also be measured in terms of Up and Down Volume.

Up Volume is the number of shares that are traded when the stock is moving in an upward or a price-increasing direction. Similar but conversely, Down Volume is the number of shares that are traded when the stock is moving in a downward or price decreasing direction.

Traders often used Up / Down Volume as a solid indicator of enthusiasm for a stock on a given day, with more enthusiasm being shown with higher Up Volume shares, with opposite true of higher Down Volume days

80.

"STOCK REPURCHASE PROGRAMS"

Stock Repurchase Programs are initiated by public companies and announced to the public at the company's discretion. In essence, these are programs where the company's Board of Directors has authorized the company to purchase its own shares on the stock market with excess cash the company possesses.

Stock Repurchase Programs are generally initiated by a company when they feel that the stock market is not fairly valuing the company, meaning the company believes its stock price is too low. So the company uses its cash to buy their stock in the market, in theory driving up the stock price by adding a large buyer of their stock: themselves.

81.

"A CATALYST"

Given its standard definition of "as a thing that drives change," a Catalyst in investing terms represents something similar as pertains to investments. It is an element or an action that precipitates movement of an investment, in either direction, solely because of that element or action.

Typical catalysts in the Investment world can be a news story or an earnings report or a geopolitical event. Often times investors are asking themselves what is the next catalyst to drive an investment, higher or lower. Many times if there is no catalyst an investment will merely drift in price, almost directionless, until some event or action occurs driving it in one direction or the other. Any investors spend time considering what the next catalyst will be.

82.

"RETRACEMENT / REVERSAL"

Very much terms of frequent traders and day traders, stock Retracements and Reversals refer to market situations where an underlying asset is returning back to a previous price level after making a strong move in some direction. Retracements and Reversals act as key indicators for many investors to either buy or sell depending on the direction of the move.

As an example, if Apple stock rises from $200 to $220, a 10% move in price, oftentimes, it will make a retracement or reversal back towards the original price level, in this case, $200. It's important to note that to be a retracement / reversal it may not make a full retracement back to the initial price, but fair to say, that a substantial move towards it constitutes this effect.

142

83.

"EXTENDED / OVEREXTENDED"

An Extended Stock or Market is a phrase that investors use to describe either a stock or a financial market, most usually the stock market, that have risen too far and too fast and to such a level that is believed beyond what is properly dictated by financial analysis.

Sometimes a stock or market rises very quickly, say increases 10% or more in a short period like a month. This will push up the price to earnings ratio of the stock or entire market and many investers will begin to think that the market is extended or even overextended. There is no set specific amount of rise that delineates extended or overextended, it is generally just a personal belief of an investor or analyst based on their experience and financial analysis.

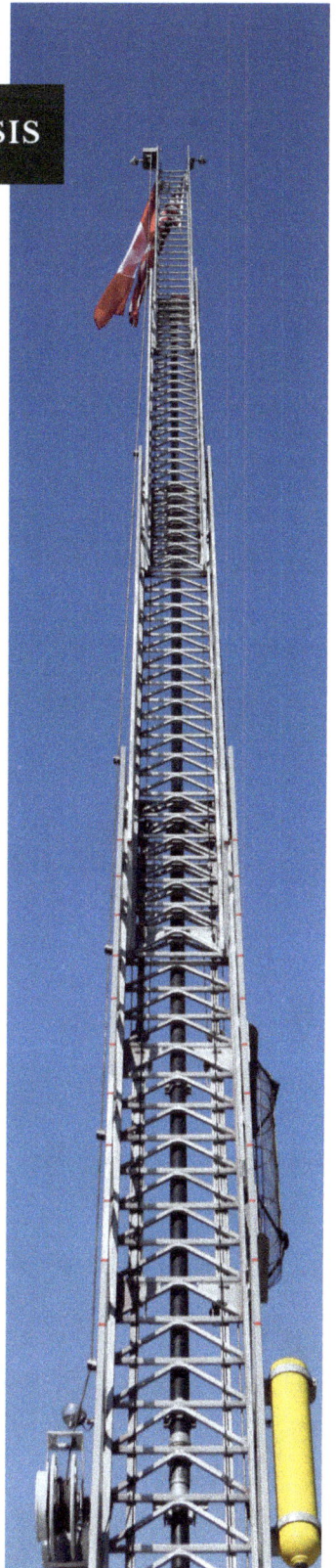

143

84.

"MARKET ROTATION"

Market Rotation is defined, in theory, as when stock investors move their buying interest from one category of stock investing to a different one. Often, this comes with the selling of the previous preferred category to use that money to buy stocks in the newly preferred category. Thus, the Investor is rotating from one category to another.

This happens very often when a country's economy switches in its economic cycle. As a country's economy rebounds, investors will often switch from value stocks to growth stocks. The opposite will occur as the economy slows. Sometimes the rotation is from large capitalization companies to small capitalization companies. The goal is to rotate to an investment sector that will do better given economic conditions.

85.

"A TIGHT STOP"

A phrase more usually associated with day traders then long-term investors, a Tight Stop is when a trader has taken a position in a financial asset, but then immediately puts in a Stop Order very close to the just effectuated purchase price. The purpose of this stop order is to substantially limit the amount of loss that the trader will have to take if the asset price moves contrary to their initial investment.

As an example, a trader buys a large amount of Apple stock at $200 hoping that it will go up to $205 very quickly. They are unwilling to risk long term losing money so they will put in a stop loss order at $198. This placing of the stop loss price just below the purchase price represents a tight stop from the trader's perspective.

86.

"CPI / PPI"

In long firm respectively, Consumer Price Index (CPI) and Producer Price Index (PPI), are measures of inflation that the Federal Government produces on a monthly basis that purport to represent what has happened to a basket of goods in terms of their prices over the last month. These reports are released by the government and are used by the Federal Reserve to help them guide monetary policy and my investors to help them make investing decisions in financial markets

Basket of goods used to compile the CPI and the PPI are consistent from month to month so that the Index figures give one an accurate gauge of what has happened to prices during the period. The release of these figures using important event each month for investing markets.

146

87.

"WASH SALE"

A Wash Sale is a sale that occurs within 30 days of a selling a stock solely for tax loss purposes. The Wash Sale rule was implemented so that investors cannot write off their losses so easily to avoid capital gains tax.

An example: A stock you bought has a loss so that you sell it. By selling it, you generate a capital loss which reduces your capital gains. If you purchase the exact same stock back less than 30 days from the previous sale, the previous sale is considered a Wash Sale. The price of the new purchase will be adjusted to account for the old sale. Note: The Wash Sale rule does not generally exist with with retirement accounts.

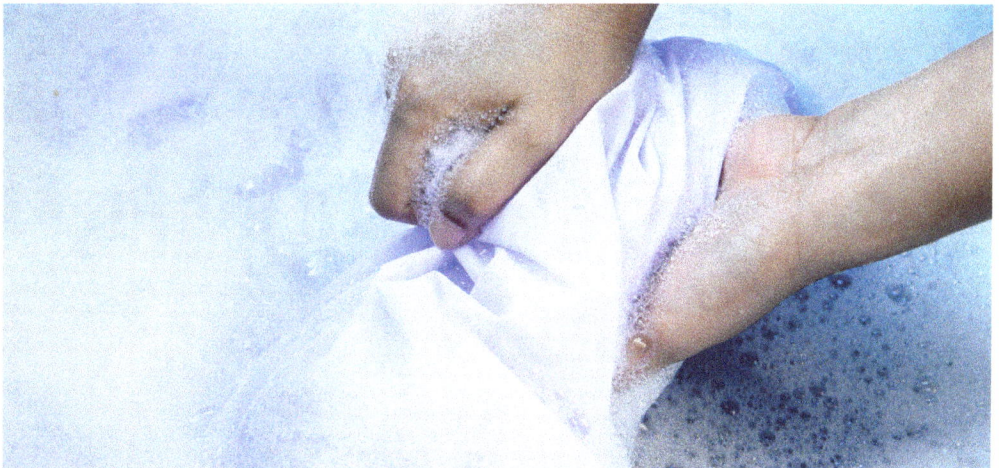

88.

"WRITING A CALL / PUT"

People understand that one can buy Call and Put options giving them the right to buy or sell at a certain price, but it is important to understand that some other party has created that option for them to buy. The creation of an option is called Writing, as in Writing a call or Writing a put.

The writing of a call or put is most often done by large financial institutions, but can be also done by individuals making a financial investment decision based on factors like where they believe the market is going, or as a reflection of holdings in their own account. In theory, someone or some Institution is always willing to write a call or put for purchase and the only unknown determinant is at what price.

INVESTING BASICS

INVESTMENT STRATEGY

ESSENTIAL INVESTING BASICS

89.

"INVESTOR PROFILE"

One's Investor Profile is an analysis and study of an investor's Risk Tolerance and Investment Horizon together. The Investor Profile gives insight into the nature of the investor's goals and objectives when it comes to investing.

The analysis often breaks down into four quadrants: high and low Risk Tolerance and long and short Investment Horizon.

It is extremely useful to know one's Investor Profile before one begins the Investment portfolio building process. It generally changes over time with changes in age and readily-investible cash amounts. In fact, it's a good idea to revisit it every 10 years, if not more often if life events warrant.

90.

"INVESTMENT HORIZON"

Investment Horizon is a key metric when developing one's profile for making investing decisions. It stands for how long an investor has the capacity to remain invested in their investments, and it adjusts over time.

For example, a young person of 25 years old, when developing an investment portfolio for retirement, has an Investment Horizon of at least 40 years (the difference between 25 and retirement age). A retired person at the age of 75 has a much shorter Investment Horizon, say ~5 years, as their life expectancy would be typically much shorter, and thus their investing period is much more limited.

One should think of their Investment Horizon when making decisions about investments, especially related to retirement.

91.

"RISK PROFILE / RISK TOLERANCE"

Along with Investment Horizon, Risk Tolerance, also known as one's Risk Profile, is a metric that measures one's ability to withstand risk and "problematic events" with their investment portfolio. In this case, problematic events can be defined as a loss of a substantial portion or all of their capital purchased for investment.

Those people with less Risk Tolerance should make sure to invest in certain asset classes that, by definition, come with lower risk such as government bonds. Those people with a higher Risk Tolerance can be more comfortable investing in assets that have a greater chance of not succeeding, such as speculative stocks and startups.

92.

"RISK ADVERSE / RISK TOLERANT"

Opposite sides of the Risk spectrum coin, Risk Averse and Risk Tolerant describe the attitude of someone to risk and the chances of a risky event affecting their business/investments.

Risk Adverse describes someone who is not interested in and even is against taking on projects, investments, etc that contain a greater than average risk profile. This means when risks are great, there is a greater than average chance of failure or loss of money.

People who are Risk Tolerant are open to taking on projects, investments etc. that are riskier than average, where the chance of failure and loss of money is not insubstantial and may be greater than average.

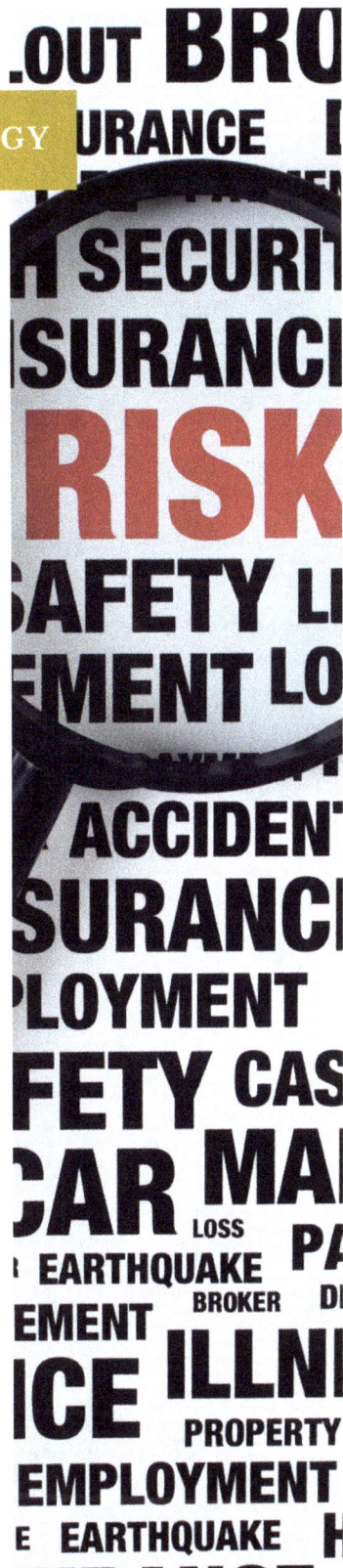

93.

"EQUITY STYLE BOX"

Developed by Morningstar, the Equity Style Box categorizes companies, but much more commonly, ETFs and mutual funds into a sector-on-a-grid analysis as seen below. It divides investible entities into sectors based on the Market Cap size (large, medium, small) and their Investing focus (value, blend, growth). It is a simple, but useful tool to compare various investment instruments for their appropriateness to one's investment portfolio.
Photo ©: Investopia

	Value	Blend	Growth
Large			■
Medium			
Small			

94.

"INVESTOR LIFECYCLE"

The Investor Lifecycle, ranging from New investor at hopefully a young age to a more evolved, diversified investor at an older age, is driven by many factors including age, work capacity, annual income, wealth, risk tolerance, health etc. In essence, the type of investor you are depends on where you are in your life cycle based on those various factors

There are several variations on how the stages or modes of investing are named but generally:
1. Capital Growth (rapid growth)
2. Capital Appreciation (slow growth)
3. Capital Sustainability (risk neutral)
4. Capital Preservation (low risk)
5. Capital Conservation (very low risk)

95.

"CAPITAL GROWTH MODE"

The average investor life cycle has different stages, and one of the most important, is the Capital Growth Mode. This is where the Investor is trying to generate returns in excess of the average market returns by taking on a substantial level of risk with their investments.

Over time, it is believed that taking on greater risk should be rewarded with achieving greater returns, because why would we take on the greater risk if not. The Capital Growth mode generally will carry higher investments in riskier assets, namely stocks, and even more specifically, speculative growth stocks versus less risky assets such as corporate and government bonds. An investor should be able to accept and survive the risks associated with this stage.

96.

"CAPITAL APPRECIATION MODE"

The average investor life cycle has different stages, and one of the most important, is the Capital Appreciation Mode. This mode is where the Investor is trying to generate returns slighter greater than the average market returns by taking on a moderate level of risk with their investments.

Over time, taking moderate risk should always be rewarded with achieving greater returns, though not outsized returns. The Capital Appreciation mode generally will carry slightly higher investments in riskier assets, namely stocks and even specifically growth stocks, versus less risky assets such as bonds. An investor should be able to accept and survive the risks associated with this stage, even though risks are moderated by design.

97.

"CAPITAL PRESERVATION MODE"

One's investor profile generally changes as one ages, mostly with people actively getting more conservative as they get closer to retirement, and eventually entering retirement, a period of life without salary generation. The Capital Preservation Mode is the first step into the territory where preserving what you have now is more important than growing what you will have tomorrow.

During the Capital Preservation phase there should be a movement of one's investments towards more Fixed Income holdings such as bonds of various different kinds (government, corporates, inflation protected,etc.) versus riskier stocks holdings. In fact, Fixed Income should become the majority of one's holdings, certainly greater than 50% and upwards towards 75%.

98.

"CAPITAL CONSERVATION MODE"

The most conservative of any phase of investing is the Capital Conservation stage, and this is where most very old people on a pension trying to live off of very limited resources should be. In fact, this mode is almost a non stock-owning mode as the inherent risks in owning stocks is too great to bear for these investors.

In Capital Conservation mode, investors should be sticking to those securities with the least risk possible, which includes keeping money in an interest bearing checking account, or at most, owning only government interest bearing securities if their cash situation permits this. Obviously, wealthier investors don't need this mode.

100.

"INSTITUTIONAL OWNERSHIP"

A stock metric followed by many investors is Institutional Ownership, which tracks the percentage of outstanding shares of a company owned by the largest financial institutions. It is delineated as a percentage of total outstanding shares, for example 30%, which represents the stock float owned by large institutions.

Institutional Ownership gives investors a solid sense of the acceptance of a company by professional money managers. Since large Investment houses employ a team of analysts, large ownership by these houses implies a certain sense of belief in the company, its worthiness for investment. This can be important for new, smaller companies.

101.

"REBALANCING THE PORTFOLIO"

Over time with investment accounts, some stock sectors or industries will no doubt succeed substantially, while others may fall disproportionately. As a result of these result fluctuations, an investor often finds themselves with too much of one sector, and not enough of some other important sector. At this point, a good investor will take the important step of Rebalancing The Portfolio.

Rebalancing consists of the hard steps of selling a portion of your stocks that have been great winners, and also simultaneously purchasing more shares in your positions that have not succeeded. This will bring one's portfolio back into balance with the original investment planning for the account with the goal of greater success over the long-term.

102.

"60-40 INVESTING"

Perhaps the most famous of all Investing models, though not necessarily the best, is what is known as the 60-40 Investing model. For decades, it was what was recommended to most investors as a prudent way to setup one's investment portfolio.

Essentially, the 60-40 Investing model is organizing one's investments into various positions whereby 60% of one's investments are in stocks and 40% of one's investments are in fixed income securities. The goal of this investing strategy is to achieve a sufficient level of diversification in a portfolio, assuring appropriate levels of both stock and bond investment in order to manage risk and growth goals. Though this is considered somewhat outdated, it is still used and often considered as a marker for money managers to compare against.

103.

"GROWTH AT A REASONABLE PRICE (GARP)"

Traditionally, growth stocks trade at high multiples of earnings, certainly higher than those of what are considered value stocks. Often times, investors are trying to find stocks that they believe are Growth at a Reasonable Price (GARP). That is, stocks that have a high growth rate of earnings, at least greater than 8% a year, but are trading at a relatively low multiple of earnings as compared to other high-growing stocks.

GARP is something of a pink unicorn in the Investing world as it really shouldn't occur. Stocks that appear to be reasonably priced yet with high growth rates either have some reason for trading so cheaply, relatively, or very soon trade higher, high enough so as to lose their perceived GARP status.

104.

"DOLLAR COST AVERAGING"

Dollar Cost Averaging is an investing approach where similar amounts are put into investments regardless of timing or the price of the investment. Over time, it will lead an averaging of higher and lower purchasing prices, which will help lead to solid investment returns.

As an example, imagine putting $200 into the stock market each month irrespective of the price of the stock market or what is happening in the broader investing market. Sometimes the $200 will be invested when stock prices are low, but other times it will be when stock prices are high. This generates an average investment price over time. This approach eliminates the attempts of investors to try to time the market (which rarely happens successfully), often generates more consistent returns.

105.

"MARKET TIMING / TIMING THE MARKET"

Market timing (aka timing the market) is an approach to investing that far too many new investors try, but over time rarely succeed at. It is based on the false belief that someone can make a decision as to when it is a good or bad time to be investing in the market. The old desire to buy low and sell high drives the belief, mistakenly, that one can Time The Market, buying at the right time AND selling at the right time. Or vice versa.

Studies show overwhelmingly that the quite vast majority of investors cannot market time effectively, often because it takes making two correct decisions: buying at the right time and then selling at the right time. Statistically the chances of making those two decisions correctly are very small.

165

106.

"BUY AND HOLD STRATEGY"

Buy and Hold Strategy is a tried and true approach to investing that acknowledges it is quite difficult to know and act at the right times, to market time that is, in the stock market.

This approach believes that it is better to buy a good company's stock or other investment and hold it through good times and bad in the overall market, unless and until the underlying story about the company has changed substantially enough.

Studies show that, despite the fact most people believe they can time the stock market, better returns are achieved with a Buy and Hold Strategy. So unless one is extremely knowledgeable and very extremely focused on stock market investing, Buy and Hold is the best strategy.

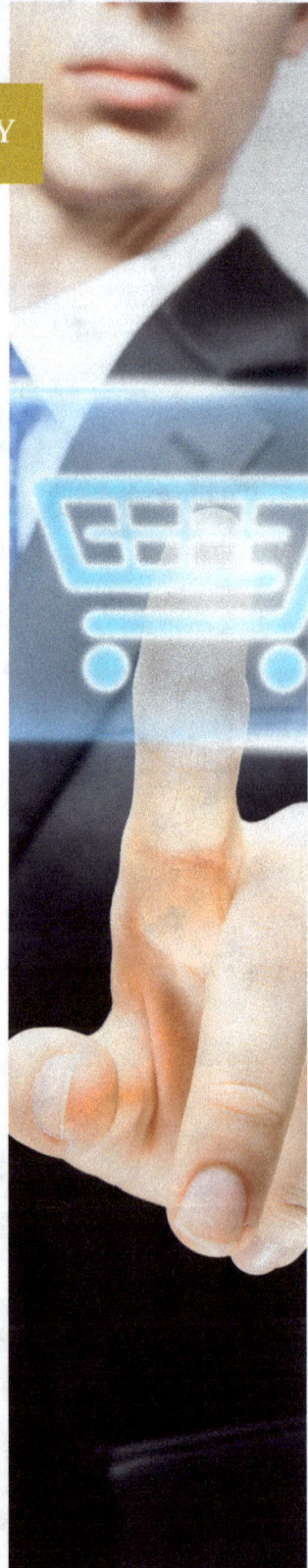

107.

"DIVERSIFICATION"

When thought of in a Financial investment context, Diversification means the spreading out of one's investments across different assets. It is "Not putting all your eggs in one basket." An investor diversifies their investments to reduce risks and it is one of the single most important actions a new investor can take.

It is very important to diversify among different assets classes, and even within asset classes; buying different industries of stocks or different bond lengths. By spreading out one's investments, you reduce the risk that one investment or area of investment wipes you out if an extraordinary event happens Think Covid and the cruise line business. If someone was all in there, they lost everything.

108.

"F.O.M.O"
(FEAR OF MISSING OUT)

One of the most consistent causes of asset bubbles and stock market crashes is FOMO, Fear Of Missing Out. How it works is simple: Some asset, usually the stock market, achieves great returns over a short period of time. Those people who have not participated in the upside because they were not invested in the stock become afraid that they will not get their share of the gains so they rush to invest. Then everyone does.

Fear Of Missing Out only feeds itself, as it propels stocks higher to absurd ranges thereby drawing more people into it until it is self-fulfilling. Until it crashes. And the last people always pay the worst price because their FOMO pushed them to enter far too late.

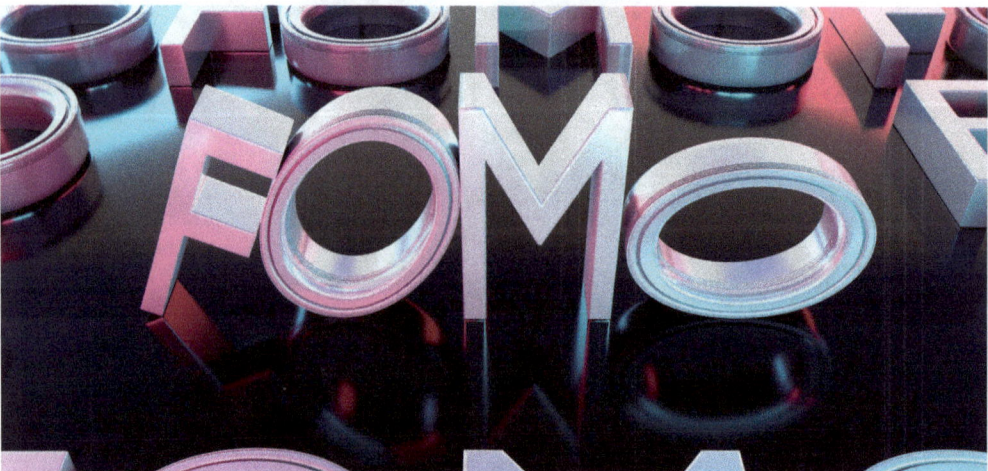

109.

"INVERSE BOND RELATIONSHIP"

One of the trickiest elements to understand in Bond investing is the famous Inverse Relationship between a bond's interest rate (yield) and its price. But while not easily intuitive, it does make perfect sense when finally it's understood correctly.

As a bond's price goes up, its yield goes down because its coupon is fixed. The coupon (nominal yield) is set when it's originated. So if its coupon is fixed, let's say at 5%, as the bond price goes up from $100 to $130, the 5% coupon is less as a percentage on the $130 price versus the $100 price. Here, price has gone up so the yield as a percentage of its price has gone down. This applies to all bonds broadly. When interest rates go up, prices on bonds with fixed yields go down. Vice versa applies here.

110.
"TAX LOSS HARVESTING"

In the United States, we pay taxes on Capital gains, the difference between what we bought an asset for and what we sold the asset for, assuming it's a positive difference. If we bought a stock for $100 and we sold it for $200, there is a capital gain of $100 and we must pay taxes on it. Sometimes we have a Capital loss where we bought it for $200 and we sold it for $100. We are allowed to write off our Capital losses against our Capital gains to reduce taxable income, thus our tax payments.

So at the end of each year, good investors do Tax Loss Harvesting, where they sell stocks that have losses to offset against stock sales with gains in the year. This lowers their taxable income, ultimately lowering their tax payments.

111.

"RELATIVE STRENGTH INDEX (RSI)"

The Relative Strength Index, known in the market as the RSI, is a much followed financial metric which helps experienced trade end invest. It is a complicated calculation that shows, as the name suggests the relative interest (or "strength") of investors for a financial asset....or the lack thereof .

Through price movements and volume analysis, the RSI shows graphically whether investors are pursuing an asset with real interest or avoiding it perhaps thoroughly. Savvy investors use the RSI to try and understand opportunities for trading, for example when to enter a stock trade or leave it. Like all popular financial indicators, they are not perfect predictors by any stretch they are only an element to help with decisions.

112.

"HERD MENTALITY"

A lot of the outsized gains that stocks sometimes achieve is attributable to Herd Mentality, a psychological term linked to members of a group all acting in similar fashion, oftentimes even without thought for the reasons why they're acting that way.

Stock market investing often shows signs of Herd Mentality related to specific stocks or specific industries within the market as a whole. A common example is when suddenly everybody is buying AI stocks or Healthcare stocks and this leads to a potentially larger than deserved movement in a stock or industry. In essence, the herd all goes one way, often without thought or reason, just as a function of everyone else doing it.With stocks this can and very badly when reason catches up with the herd.

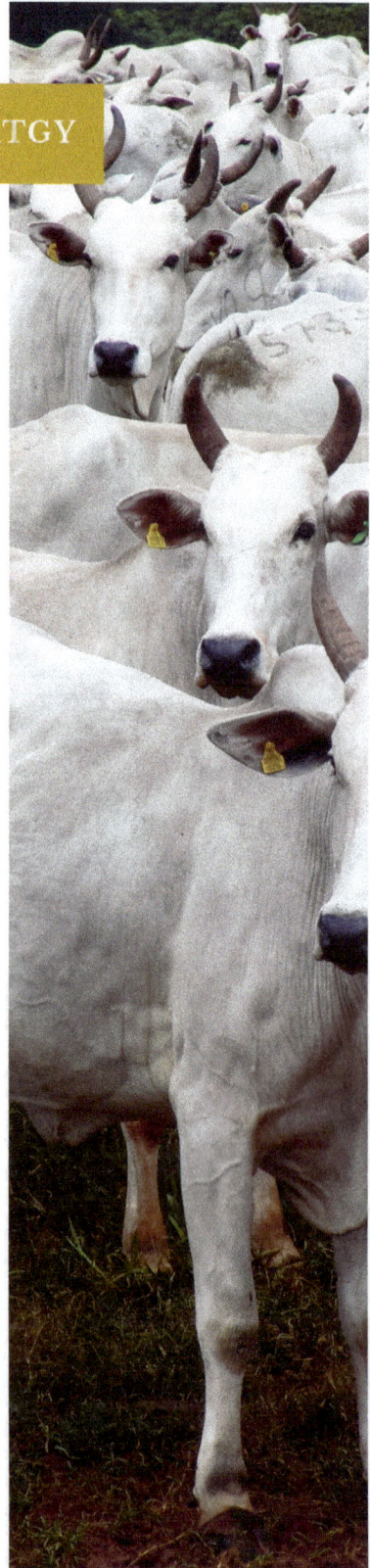

INVESTING BASICS

TRADING & STRATEGY

ESSENTIAL INVESTING BASICS

113.

"PRICED IN"

The stock market is said to be a discounting mechanism, taking into account relevant information out in the world and factoring this information into a stock price. An often-used phrase is Priced In, which means in essence that someone using the phrase believes that all the information available publicly is known and reflected in the current stock price.

For example, let's say Apple has announced a new phone service and the stock jumps 5% that day. Someone could say that the information, a new phone service, has now been Priced In to the stock price. It is important to note that Priced In is a subjective belief and never ever an objective fact. Oftentimes, one investor will believe that some information is priced in "fully" while another investor believes it is not. That makes a market.

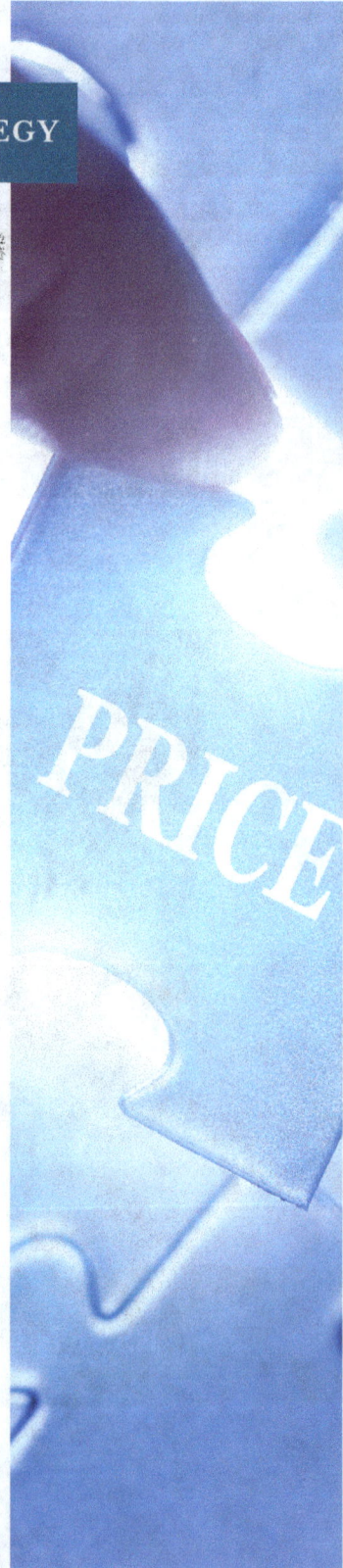

114.

"SOURCE OF FUNDS"

Source of Funds in investing is a term of art where an investor sells one of their holdings so that they can purchase another investment in its place. In this scenario, the selling of the first stock become a Source of Funds, free usable cash, for the purchase of the second stock.

For example, let's say that an Investor wants to be buy Apple stock but does not have enough free, not-invested cash in their account to buy the amount they want. The investor can sell some or all of their shares in Google to then make the wanted Apple investment. In this instance, we would say that the Google stock sale became a Source of Funds for the Apple purchase. This happens often in the market as rebalancing or opinion-changing occurs.

175

115.

"POUNDING THE TABLE"

Pounding the Table is a phrase used in the financial industry to represent when big Wall Street financial analysts are promoting hard a stock idea for investment. When a Financial analyst recommends very highly a stock they follow, to the point where they put out a press release known as a research note, it is said that the analyst is Pounding The Table on that stock.

It is important to note that just because the analyst has pounded the table on a stock, that is no guarantee that the stock's price will increase, neither because the analyst has pounded the table nor for the reasons why the analyst has pounded the table. It is merely their opinion that they are promoting forcefully.

116.

"JAWBONING"

One of the most effective tools that the Federal Reserve has in its toolbox to effect the market is the idea of Jawboning, which it uses quite often especially in periods when interest rate changes are coming.

In essence, the Federal Reserve board is made up of Federal Reserve governors, and from time to time, these governors including the Fed Chairman, will give interviews for television and newspapers speeches to organizations that push their views on what investors should expect in Fed policy. The effect of this Jawboning, stating its position publicly, is to correct misconceptions among investors as to future policy planning. These "friendly commentaries" are very effective at moving the stock market in accordance with Fed wishes.

117.

"CONSUMER CONFIDENCE"

One of the most important pieces of information that seasoned investors follow is the Consumer Confidence report which is a metric that expresses the relative confidence that consumers have in the US economy. This report is produced by The Conference Board, a non-profit research organization.

Consumer-based purchases drive the majority of the United States economy, so it stands to reason that Consumer Confidence about how the economy will fare in the future is an extremely telling metric to follow. If confidence is poor that the economy will do well, history shows that consumers tend to spend less. Conversely, optimism about the economy leads to higher spending and generally higher stock prices.

118.

"MARKET FORCES"

Broadly defined as all things that can affect a stock or a stock market, Market Forces is a catch-all term used frequently by market analysts. At its base, it's a byword for Supply and Demand dynamics and all global factors and elements affecting a stock price.

Such factors as the supply of product, quantities available, positioned against the market demand for the product, consumer interests. It is always important to remember that the stock market is ultimately just a market for stocks. And like a market for tomatoes, as with everything else, sometimes it's merely the desire / demand for a stock versus how available it is, reflecting in the price at which it is selling in a given moment of time.

119.

"TAKING A POSITION / STARTER POSITION"

A Position, often phrased as Taking A Position, is when an investor first buys an asset for investment, for instance a stock. When one buys, say, 10 shares of Apple Inc., one has taken a position in Apple. It does not necessarily need to be a long position (buying), it can be a short position (selling). Both are equally Taking A Position.

A Starter Position is when an investor initially makes a small investment in an asset with the intention of making a larger investment in the future, hopefully at a more attractive price. While the future purchase is not guaranteed nor forecasted to a certain day, often investors will take their Starter Position with a plan for future purchases to increase their overall position size.

120.

"MEAN REVERSION"

Mean Reversion is an often used phrase in Stock investing though its basis is as a mathematical concept. It speaks to the expectation that over time, numbers being tracked will return to their long-term average. As pertains to stock markets as well as individual stocks, Mean Reversion is the concept that a market or stock will return to its long term average trajectory or PE ratio if it's had a period of movement outside of its normal course, be it to the upside or downside.

As an example: Imagine a stock that has returned 20% during a 6-month time period when the overall market has improved only 3% growth. Over time, one could expect, but not definitely, that the stock will fall to become more inline with how the broader stock market is doing. This return to the average of the market is Mean Reversion.

121.

"CONTRARIAN INDICATOR"

A Contrarian Indictor, as the phrase suggests, is a market sign that runs in contradiction to what the rest of the market indicators are suggesting, or what one would think normally. Contrarian Indicators often are early warning signs that the stock market has gotten a little out of whack in either direction.

For example, a famous Contrarian Indicator is polls showing the general public is bullish on the stock market. Historically, when these polls show too much optimism, too much belief that the market is in a good place and will go higher, it has often been when a market tends to fall. This poll of optimism is a Contrarian Indicator, something one would think is positive (bullishness), but is in fact potentially negative.

122.

"WINDOW DRESSING"

Window Dressing is the practice some stock brokers / money managers have of buying certain stocks and selling others just before the close of a reporting period, like for instance, a quarter end where client statements will be produced.

In effect, because an Investment Account statement is produced and sent to the client, the broker makes the account look better by adding the right stocks in the account and removing the wrong stocks (those that generated a loss, for example) just before the statement is locked in. Window Dressing is really a manner of obfuscating poor results by removing bad investments from the statement while showing the holdings in a better light by showing that the account owns the recent "hot" stocks that have been publicized.

:turn on Investment

od Comparison

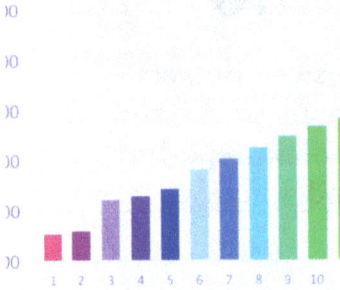

Item	Cost Per Item	Percent Markup	T...
1	$4.00	90.00%	
2	$5.00	90.00%	
3	$13.00	65...	
4	$11.50	75.00%	
	$10.00	100.00%	
6	$13.27	95.67%	
7	$14.51	98.24%	
8	$15.75	100.81%	
9	$17.00	103.38%	
10	$18.24	103.38%	
	$18.24	108.52%	
12	$20.72	111.10%	
13		...00%	
14	$22.56	114.22%	
15	$25.34	120.04%	
16	$26.72	122.95%	

al

123.

"ALPHA / CREATING ALPHA"

Derived from the Greek letter, Alpha, Creating Alpha is a term used in stock market circles to describe generating investment returns greater than the overall market (or some other relevant, appropriately used metric) when accounting for risk. It is something that all Money Managers are trying to do and it's something they use to defend their high management fees.

As an example, if the stock market return in a year is 10%, and a money manager has produce returns of 20%, while keeping risk constant, this money manager (or even a particular investment) is considered to have Created Alpha of 10%. Keeping risk constant is an important element because we don't want them buying lottery tickets.

124.

"BETA"

Beta, taken from the Greek letter and its usage in mathematics, represents a measure of variation in movement from some consistent metric. In finance, it allows two stocks to be compared to each other. It is a measure of volatility in a stock comparing it to the market as a whole.

As an example in the investing world, the S&P500 is the constant metric, and as a result it is represented by the number 1. Those stocks with a Beta greater than one, let's say 1.5, implies that this stock will move 1.5% for every 1% movement in the S&P500. A stock with a Beta of .5 will move only .5% when the S&P500 moved 1%. Those stocks with higher Betas are statistically more volatile as they move greater when the broad market moves, and vice versa for low Beta stocks.

125.

"TALKING YOUR OWN BOOK"

Something to be wary of when watching market pundits on stock news channels is them Talking Their Own Book. This is when someone touts their own holdings, that is stocks they already own, recommending others purchase what they already have a financial position in. This practice of suggesting what is own is legal and not always acknowledged.

It is important to recognize that people have biases, and often their biases are influenced by where they have invested their own money. Oftentimes you will hear financial advisors, as a sort of disclaimer, mention that they are Talking Their Own Book, or that they have positions in the stock, which they should do. It means that they are recommending something that they have a financial interest in.

126.

"ASSET BUBBLES"

Asset Bubbles occur when a mania sets in for the purchasing of some asset, usually stocks on an exchange, but not always. The most famous Asset Bubble was a Tulip craze in Holland in the 17th century. Yes, the plant. Tulips.

However despite the tulip fiasco, the most common Asset Bubble is either stocks or housing. The 21st century created two vicious Asset Bubbles in its first 10 years with the internet stock market bubble in the years 1998-2001 and then the housing bubble from years 2004-2007.

Each ended extremely painfully for so many lives with savings wiped out. So beware. Absurd things happen, and bad timing due to ignorance can be life-changingly painful.

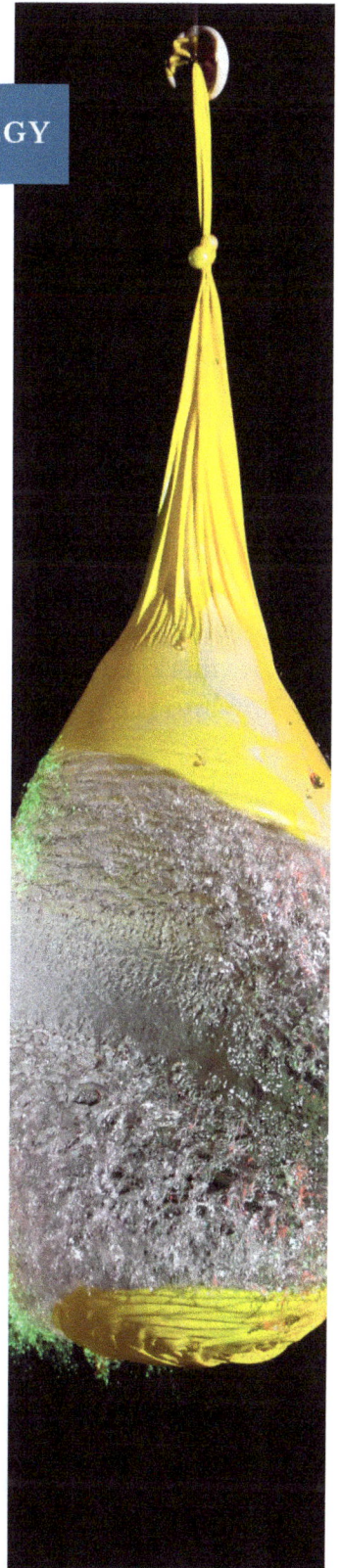

127.

"VOLATILITY INDEX (THE VIX)"

The Volatility Index is a calculated market indicator that measures perceived volatility in the financial markets. It is a much followed metric that most market insiders watch and track looking for insights into the next potential moves in the stock market.

Without getting into the calculation, it is important to understand that the higher the Volatility Index, known colloquially as the VIX, the ticker symbol, the higher perceived volatility in the market, i.e. riskiness. Conversely, the lower the VIX, the lower the perceived volatility in the market. Oftentimes, the VIX is a contraindicator, when it's too low, it's a sign of complacency and a point for caution. When it's too high, it's a sign of panic, and perhaps an opening.

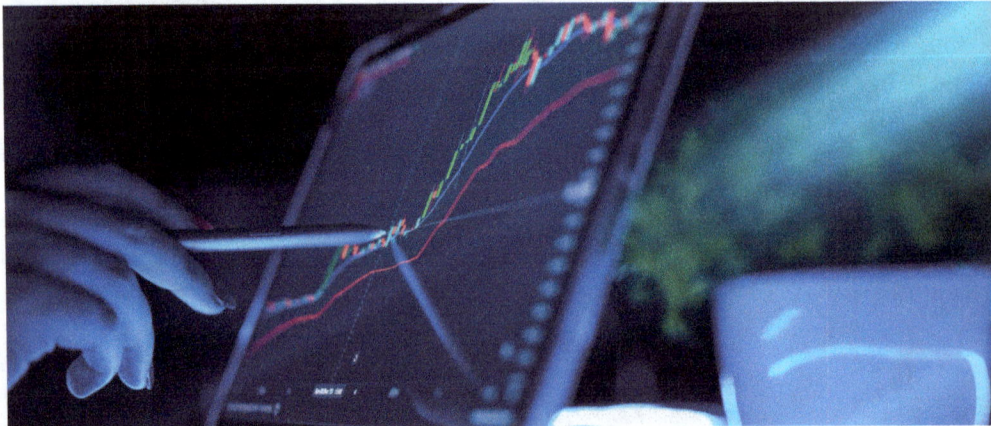

128.

"BASIS POINTS (BIPS)"

Both these phrases, Basis Points and its nickname Bips, are how seasoned stock investors speak of a hundredth of a percent. Normally it pertains to bond prices, interest rates and like denominated instruments. It's very in-the-know lingo, but not particularly useful overall.

As an example, let's say that one bond is trading at 102.65 and another similar bond is trading at 102.85. In fact, the second bond is trading at 20 Basis Points higher than the 1st bond. You can also say that the 2nd bond is 20 Bips higher than the first. Now you're in the know so you can talk to your stock broker as a professional and not a novice.

129.

"EFFICIENT MARKETS THEORY"

Efficient Markets Theory proposes the belief that the price of a financial security effectively represents most or all of the publicly available information that should affect the price of that security. There are variations in the theory (strong, semi-strong, weak) and they factor in different levels of knowledge perfection and how information affects asset prices.

The implication of this theory: If one believes that markets are efficient market mechanisms, one accepts that it's not possible to gain any advantage over other investors from either fundamental or technical asset analysis because the market price is always the correct price given all the available information. It argues for a long-term Buy and Hold strategy.

130.

"DEAD CAT BOUNCE"

This charming trader phrase, Dead Cat Bounce, describes a very specific situation in stock markets. Essentially, it occurs after a substantial fall in the markets has occurred, usually a bear market that is represented by a minimum 20% drop from a market high point.

The Dead Cat Bounce occurs when the market has a healthy rise from the bottom, sometimes a very quick one, over a few days even, but then falls back down towards its lows, and potentially makes a lower low. In essence, the Dead Cat Bounce is a fake rise that doesn't hold, but sucks in a bunch of people into believing that a new Bull market has begun. It is a bit graphic of an image, but effective.

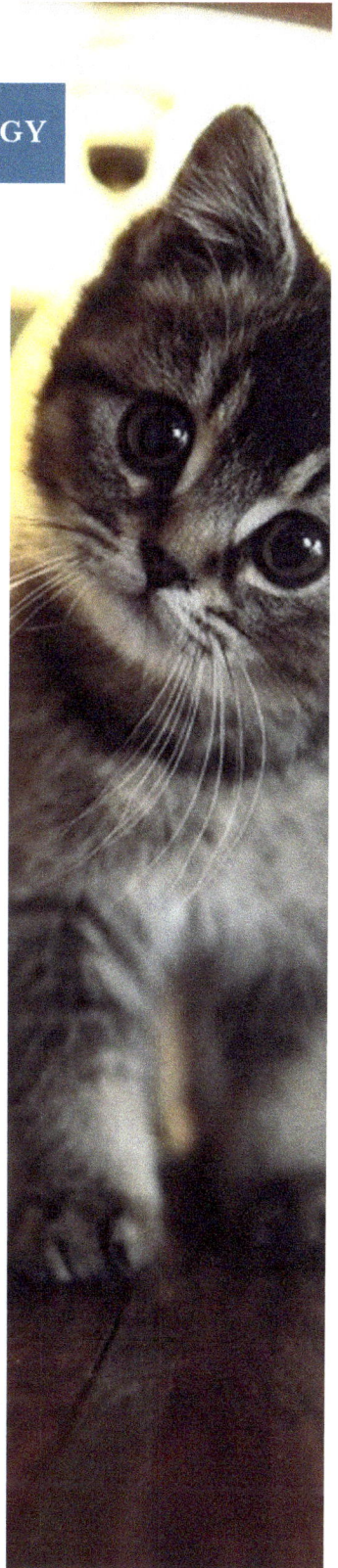

131.

"CARRY TRADE"

A Carry Trade is an attempt to capitalize on interest rate differences in different markets, especially different countries. It consists of borrowing money in one country with a low interest relative to another country, and investing that money in some financial asset, very often stocks. And not necessarily in stocks in the market in which the money was borrowed.

An example: Imagine the Interest rate in Japan is 1% and it's 5% in the United States. One can borrow money in Japan, with certain requirements met, and then invest it in the US to get the higher interest rate. This is profitable if the currency rate between the two countries is not too reactive. But pay attention, this is a risky strategy, and can unwind painfully if currency or interest rates don't act as one expects.

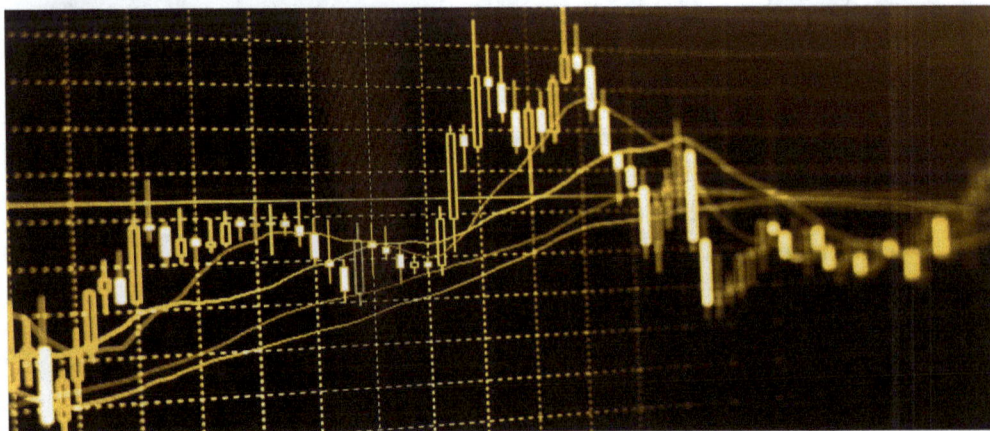

132.

"MARKET TOP / MARKET BOTTOM"

These important phrases are how experienced market participants speak of stock market highs and stock market lows for a given period of time. The seasoned investor will often use these as reference points to help make trading decisions.

In essence, a Top or a Bottom represents the extreme number that the stock market hits during its current phase of movement, the point thereafter that the market moved in the opposite direction. Obviously, a Market Top is the highest point the market hit in its current movement higher, just before declining, and conversely, a Market Bottom represents the lowest point the market hit before rising higher off of that point.

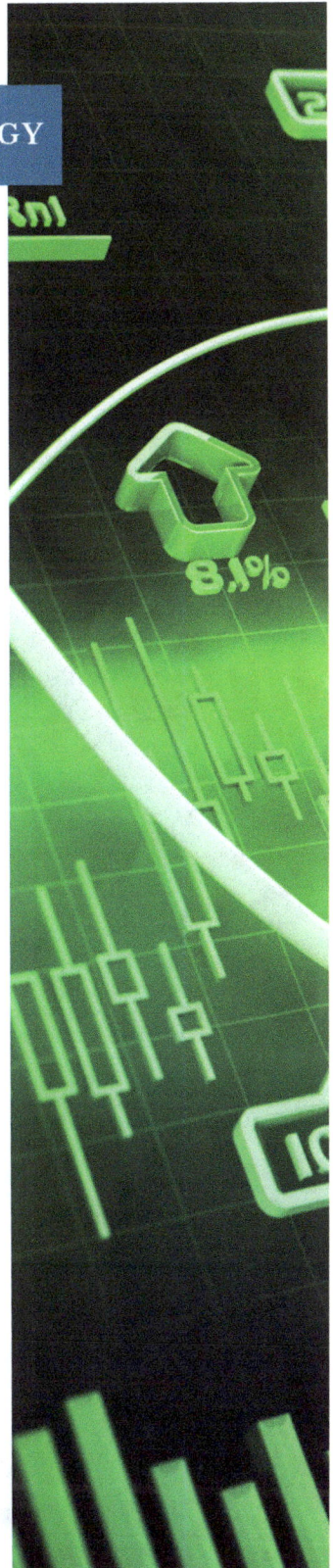

133.

"RETESTING THE LOWS"

Historically, but not always, when a stock market has a substantial drop, be it a correction or worse, a bear market, the stock market indices (S&P500, Nasdaq) will often do what is known as Retesting The Lows. This is where a bottom may have been hit, and the market has risen off it, sometimes as much as 10%.

However many experienced traders, relying on Technical Analysis, will expect that the market will go back down near the previous low (the supposed bottom), and retest whether there is real market interest in buying at that lower limit. Sometimes, a market will Retest The Low multiple times before traders feel confident that a solid bottom is in.

134.

"EMERGING MARKETS VS. DEVELOPED MARKETS"

Investors use different words to categorize various country's stock markets outside the United States, each one having their own investible stock market. Developed Markets, the name somewhat arrogant in its assumption, refers to those countries where their stock markets are very well established and have been in existence for very long periods of time, let's say more than 100 years. Developed Markets tend to be the Western countries in Europe and America.

Emerging Markets is the category that houses all the rest of the countries of the world, from giant countries like China and Russia to smaller countries like Saudi Arabia and Latin American countries. These countries have stock markets that are less established over time so the word "emerging" is used to describe them.

135.

"PROGRAM / QUANTITATIVE / ALGORITHMIC TRADING"

It is impossible to overstate the power of computers on daily trading in both stock and bond markets. While there are slight variations in each, Program Trading, often called Quantitative Trading and even Algorithmic Trading, is where large investments are made based on precise, intricate computer models that have been designed and that trigger instantaneously when certain metrics are met in the marketplace.

Example: A computer program can be written that automatically purchases a large quantity of shares in a stock if on the Thursday after a Fed meeting when the price drops 1% and trading is light. This trading has the power to move the entire market because of the speed, precision, and volume of action.

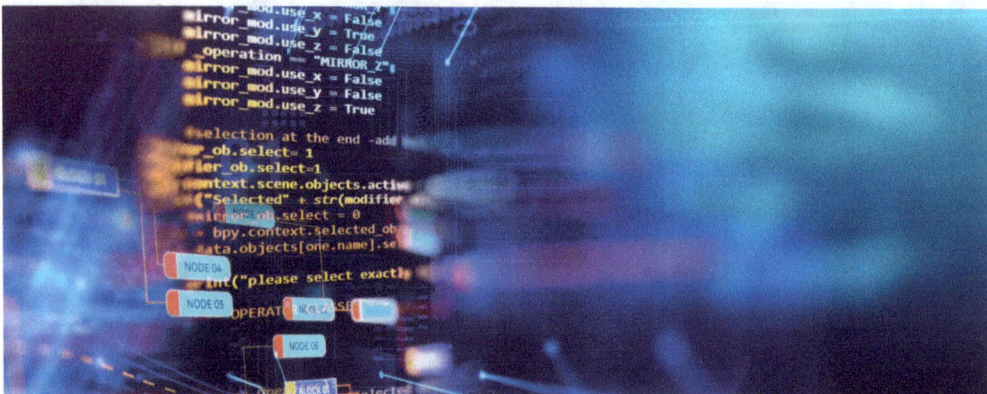

136.

"INSIDER TRADING"

Insider Trading is a crime whereby someone uses "inside" private, material information to make trading decisions, be it buying or selling. As it's a crime, it is punishable by jail time. In fact, famous people have gone to jail for it. Martha Stewart being one.

There are very specific laws that delineate what firmly constitutes Insider Trading, but in general, making buy / sell decisions based on information that is both not publicly available and important is illegal. Certainly, employees and people tangentially related to a company's management trading on such non-public information would be illegal. In certain circumstances, someone overhearing a discussion at a bar and trading on that information could also be illegal. So be careful and play it straight.

137.

"INSIDER BUYING / SELLING"

Very different from the previous page's entry, Insider Buying and Selling is legal and is a very followed, and often a stock-price moving metric. In fact, in the industry, there are weekly reports about Insider Buying and Selling, and often times there are press releases tied to it.

Insider Buying and Selling is when someone who is a part of the management team, broadly defined, makes legal sales or purchases of their company's stock. From time to time all members of the management of a company will need to buy or sell some stock for their own personal uses and reasons. Oftentimes Insider Buying is seen as a endorsement for the company, and conversely, right or wrong, Insider Selling is seen as a bad commentary on a stock.

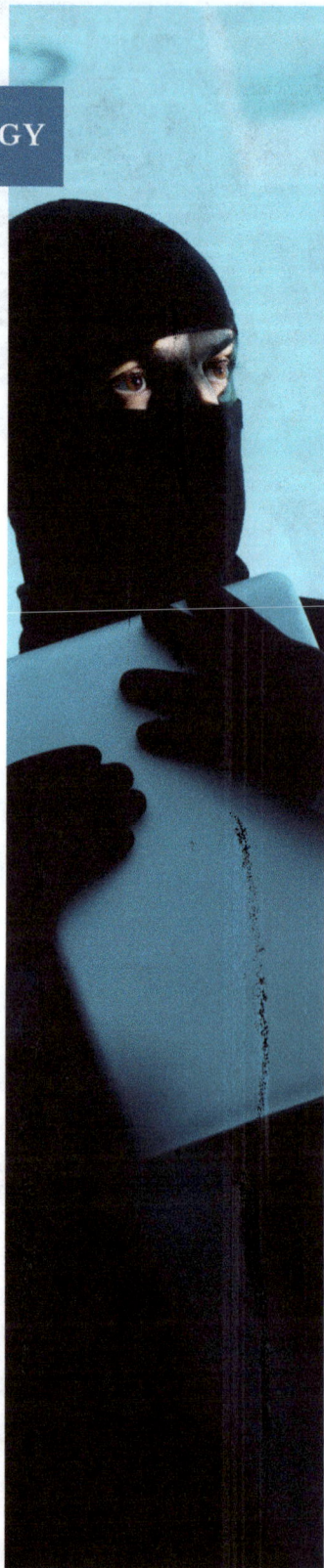

138.

"CYCLICAL VS. NON-CYCLICAL STOCKS"

With publicly traded stocks there are many different classifications that exist, all with a goal of differentiating them into useful categories. One of the more useful is Cyclical versus Non-Cyclical stocks.

Basically, Cyclical Stocks are those whose success are very tied to a growing economy versus Non-Cyclical Stocks which tend to be successful regardless of whether the economy is doing well or in a slowdown. Classic examples of Cyclical Stocks are industrial companies like steel and farming equipment stocks. When the economy is good, these companies do very well. Conversely, consumer staple companies, those selling soda, toilet paper, do well irrespective of the economy as people need these products either way.

139.

"BUY SIDE VS. SELL SIDE"

A common distinction between the various participants in the financial industry is whether they are on what's known as the Buy Side or the Sell Side of the industry. Sometimes this can be an important distinction when one is looking at financial research reports and understanding who produced it.

The Buy Side are those companies who buy financial instruments such as investment managers, pension funds etc. Their main function is buying securities. Sell Side are those financial companies that sell financial instruments such as investment banks, who represent companies bringing their stock to market. Occasionally it is interesting to know who is giving the research as they have different objectives and perspectives. Some firms do both sides of the line.

140.

"DEFAULT RISK"

In theory, inherent in the price of every Bond that is traded publicly on the market is what is known as Default Risk, the possibility that the government or company will not make the required payments to the bondholders. This can include the interest payments due as well as the return of principal payments made at the end of the bond term.

As one would expect, Default Risk increases as one buys bonds of less and less secure, healthy entities. Government Bonds from the United States are the most secure bond in the world, with the lowest Default Risk. Going further down the chain, smaller companies and companies financially in trouble represent the highest risk for Default, and thus must pay a higher interest rate for an investor to take on risk and buy their bond.

141.

"REINVESTMENT RISK"

In theory, there is an element of Reinvestment Risk in all bonds that are traded publicly. Specifically it is the risk that bondholders bear which implies that the future Interest rate one will be able to reinvest their Bond principle may be lower than what it is today.

If one has a bond paying 6% annually for 10 years and interest rates have fallen substantially, one must know that when the principle is returned, they will not be able to reinvest that money at an equally high interest rate without taking on considerably more risk. This fact may effect one's decision to hold the bond until term or whether to sell it early, given one's investment objectives.

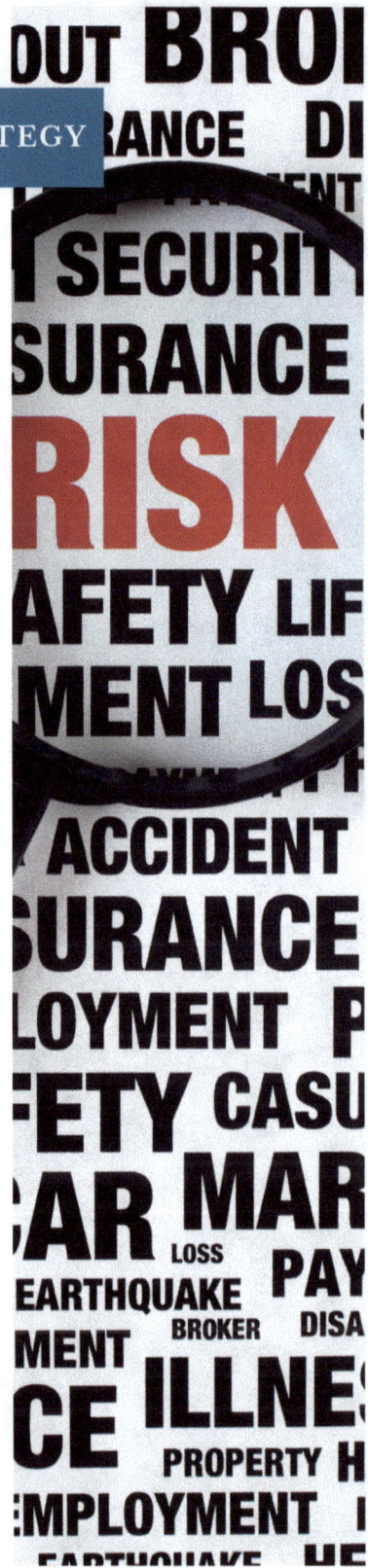

142.

"EQUAL WEIGHTED VS. MARKET CAPITALIZATION WEIGHTED"

There are two main but different ways to design the investments in a stock fund that is tied to an index; one is Equal Weighted and the other is Market Capitalization weighted. An Equal Weighted Fund will hold the same amount of investments in each stock that makes up that index. Let's say, a Billion dollars of each of the 100 stocks.

A Market Capitalization Weighted Fund will hold investments of the stocks in the index in relative size to their Market Capitalization. So if one stock has a market capitalization of twice another stock, the fund will have twice the investment of the larger capitalization stock versus the relatively smaller cap stock.

143.

"AN EXPENSIVE / INEXPENSIVE MARKET"

This is one of the most common phrases you will hear from the talking heads on the financial channels: "The market is expensive" or more rarely, "The market is inexpensive." What the speaker is talking about is the Price to Earnings ratio of the stocks in the S&P 500.

It is possible to calculate all the earnings divided by all the shares to get an earnings per share for the S&P 500 companies. From that, you can derive a price earnings multiple that the overall market is trading at. Historically the market trades somewhere between a 15 to 19 times multiple of its price to earnings. So when the market is trading at a 20+ multiple, many people will say that the market is expensive. When it is under 15, which is rare, people will talk of it as inexpensive.

144.

"CULT STOCKS"

More a modern phenomenon that has resulted from the social media takeover of investing, Cult Stocks are those highly publicized stocks where their notoriety and trading activity is often outsized as compared to their capacity to generate real profits. These stocks can range from giant companies to much smaller stocks that fit some particular niche.

In essence with Cult Stocks, either trading activity or retail ownership is extreme, beyond what may be warranted. This occurs because sometimes day traders are gambling on a stock's next direction (Tesla), or also sometimes because belief in a stock's future becomes almost biblical (Apple). Either reason is validated by high trading and/or investment activity, and it is not necessarily valid stock analysis.

145.

"INFLATION PROTECTED BONDS"

Inflation Protected Bonds are debt instruments whose interest payments adjust based on the rate of inflation in the country that sells them. They can be perhaps excellent conservative investments for shareholders who want to limit their risk to inflation.

The goal of many who buy Inflation Protected Bonds is to keep their purchasing power relatively the same, irrespective of what happens with inflation. If inflation goes up, the bonds pay larger interest payments. Vice versa, if inflation lowers, the bonds pay lower amounts to the bondholders. It is important to note that the price of the bonds also adjust with inflation rates but this is governed by the market.

146.

"CHASING THE MARKET"

One of the easiest ways of losing money in the stock market, Chasing The Market, is when you are buying stocks late, after a broad stock market rally has already made a huge run higher. It is the classic mistake, and everyone makes it. Too often.

Chasing The Market occurs because of FOMO, fear of missing out. We buy too late because we get excited and optimistic because the market has been going much higher and perhaps we didn't participate in the big run as much as we would have liked. It is the big run higher that creates the optimism, so we don't want to miss it. However, we buy too late without recognizing our optimism was greater than our prudence.

147.

"MARGIN / GOING INTO MARGIN"

Margin, or going into margin, is when one borrows money against their investment portfolio. Some investment houses allow an investor who has substantial and sufficient investment holdings to borrow against their investment holdings held at the firm. This borrowing of money beyond your cash balance is going into margin, and there will be an interest fee paid on the margin amount.

Investors need to be careful when using margin or going into margin to finance their investments in financial markets. An adverse drop in the financial assets will force the Investment bank to make a margin call which could force the Investor to liquidate their holdings at a bad moment to reduce the amount of margin they have.

148.

MARGIN REQUIREMENTS"

All firms that allow clients to use Margin have what is known as Margin Requirements, which is a calculation of the amount of value in investment holdings the account must have in order to maintain a margin loan. The Margin Requirement varies to the person, and to the type, quality and value of the holdings in the account.

For example, certain financial assets can be borrowed against at a higher rate than others based on how secure that asset is. United States Government bonds being the most secure asset. Additionally certain stocks are considered less risky than other stocks, and thus people are allowed a higher level of margin, borrowing capacity, than they are with the more risky stocks.

MARGIN

149.

"STOCK BUYBACKS"

A factor that affects individual stocks over a period of time, and are happily received by the market, Corporate Stock Buybacks are when a company listed on a stock exchange purchases its own stock with its available cash in the open market. It is a synonym for Stock Repurchase Programs.

Corporate Stock Buybacks are viewed favorably by the market because, in real essence, it's a statement of confidence that the company's making. They believe their stock price does not represent the true value of their company. When you think about it, a company would not buy back its stock if it thought it was too expensive or overvalued so the Buyback is a statement of confidence in the company by the company.

150.

"INITIAL PUBLIC OFFERINGS (IPO)"

Initial Public Offerings often abbreviated as IPOs, are when a company sells some of its shares in the company on a public stock exchange for the very first time. It is usually a very happy day for the company's first private shareholders, the early investors and founders as it is a sign of maturity and acceptance.

There is a long and complicated process for getting listed on one of the major stock exchanges, the NASDAQ and New York Stock Exchange, and this distinction is not offered to every Small company. Companies must have a certain level of sales and cash solvency to be afforded the right. After IPO has occurred, which is the selling of shares to the public, the company will trade as a normal stock on the exchange

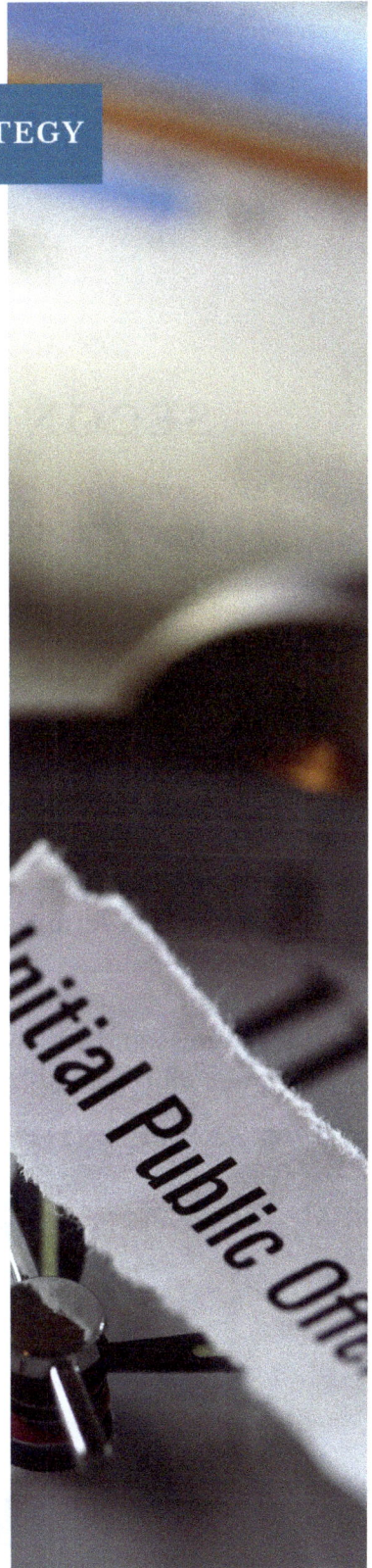

151.

"SECONDARY OFFERING"

As a company's cash flow needs warrant it, a company will from time to time raise cash by selling additional shares to the public market. This is known as a Secondary Offering, as it is not the initial public offering (IPO).

Many times, Secondary Offerings are not well received by stock markets, though this is not always the case. Generally, Secondary Offerings dilute the existing shares as the company's profits, which don't change because of the offering, but are now split over a larger number of shares. By definition this lowers the earnings per share. It also represents the fact that the company perhaps cannot generate enough cash internally to grow its business and stay afloat. Thus, often it is worrisome, and not well received by the market.

152.

"RETAIL VS. INSTITUTIONAL STOCK OWNERSHIP"

Retail Ownership of stocks is defined as when the average person owns stocks in their private accounts. They are the "Retail" Investor. This differs from Institutional Stock Ownership, which is defined by stocks held in the accounts of large financial industry companies such as Goldman Sachs, JP Morgan etc.

Institutional versus Retail Ownership of a company's stock is a statistic that is very-closely followed by Wall Street analysts. As these two different categories of investors have different goals and expertise, it can shed some light on the stock and its risk profile. In theory, but not always in practice, Institutional Investors are better at investing over the long term than their Retail counterparts so their participation is well received.

153.

"BUYING THE DIP"

Perhaps the greatest stock strategy of all time, Buying The Dip has the greatest record of any other strategy. Buying The Dip is buying stocks, or the stock market as a whole, when it has dropped some substantial amount. The Dip, per se, is the drop in stock prices.

Generally, a Dip starts around a 5% drop in the market, but sometimes it's just 3-4%. Certainly a 10% correction qualifies. The key is having some courage to start stepping in with some purchasing of the stocks when these thresholds are met. While Buying The Dip can be done on an individual stock basis, for the most part, it is related to the broader stock market as a whole as represented by the S&P 500, or the NASDAQ.

154.

"MARKET DISLOCATIONS"

In finance, Market Dislocations is a fancy way of saying that the market has in its activity, mispriced temporarily an asset price. Of course, this is personal opinion and not a verifiable fact, as all prices act in a supply and demand world. As an investor we look for market dislocations, what we believe are mispriced assets, as an opportunity to make an investment.

Sometimes a news story can drive Dislocations, in the market as a whole or in a specific investment like a stock. During these instances, an exaggerated response has occurred to some news story, in either direction positive or negative. Then the price of the asset does not reflect an appropriate value and an opportunity arises.

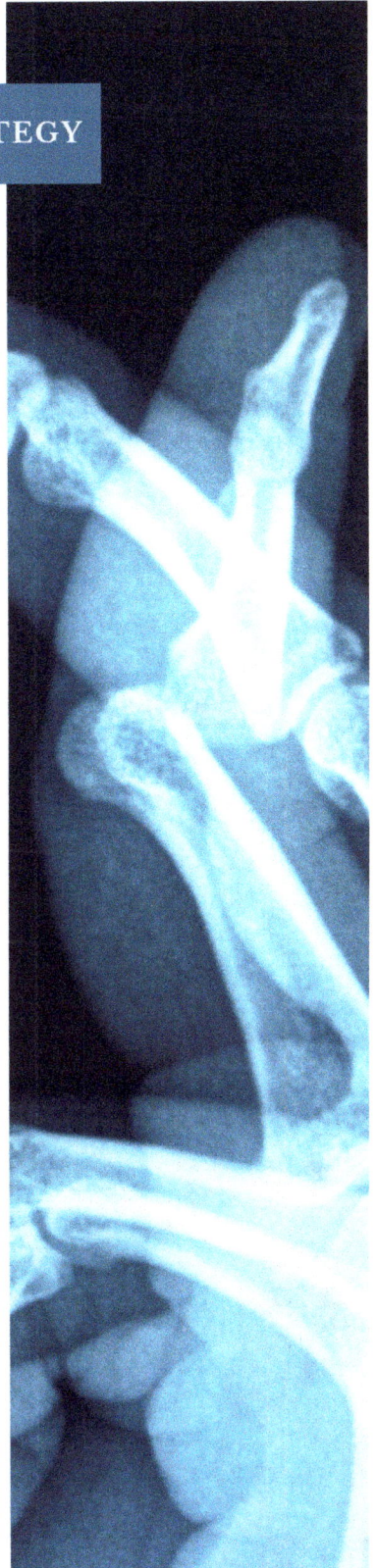

215

155.

"RISK ON VS. RISK OFF"

Risk On and Risk Off are phrases that seasoned investors use to describe the action in a stock market in terms of where investors are putting their money to work. Inherently, there are stocks of certain companies that are more risky than others, for example, a giant utility stock versus a new AI technology stock.

A Risk On market is describing a market where investors are investing in more riskier stocks, faster growing but higher multiple stocks than normal. Conversely, a Risk Off market describes a market where investors are taking money out of riskier stocks and put it into more stable, slow growth stocks like utilities and consumer staples. The Risk designation is not a formal thing, but merely a descriptor used to explain how a market is reacting during a period.

156.

"NON-FARM PAYROLLS"

This essential government statistic, which is released on the first Friday of every month, is a measure of how many jobs were created or lost in the previous month in the United States. It is one of the biggest Investment market movers on a consistent basis as it tends to effect all elements of both financial and monetary policy.

The total number excludes jobs related to farming because they are very seasonal and fluctuate greatly depending on the month. The number does include both public and private sector created jobs, which means federal and local government hiring is including in and often substantially affects the numbers. All investment market participants should follow what is happening with this number on a monthly basis. It's that important since to economic health.

157.

"DAY TRADER VS. INVESTOR"

With the difference here, it all comes down to time frame and profitability goals.

A Day Trader is someone who takes positions for very short periods of time, usually at most, a couple of days, but often just a few hours or even minutes. They are looking for very small movements in an asset, say from $30 to $30.20 in a stock price and will make the quick buy and sale to capture that small incremental profit. Though the profit is only .8%, the time frame may have been an hour or a day.

By contrast, Investors are those who hold their positions for long periods of time, buying shares in companies they believe have a bright futures to generate profits over long periods.

218

158.

"DEFENSIVE STOCKS"

Defensive Stocks represent a group of stocks in industries that do not swing wildly with economic news or even changes in the economic environment. They are generally larger company stocks that pay a solid dividend that are not particularly reactive to economic changes.

Some of the classic Defensive Stock industries are utilities, defense, and consumer staples companies such as soda and hygiene product companies. The theory being here that even in bad economic times, the public will still need to buy and pay for their utilities and staples like food, toilet paper, and soap. And historically, Defensive Stocks do well "relatively" in a prolonged, or severe challenging economic environment like recessions.

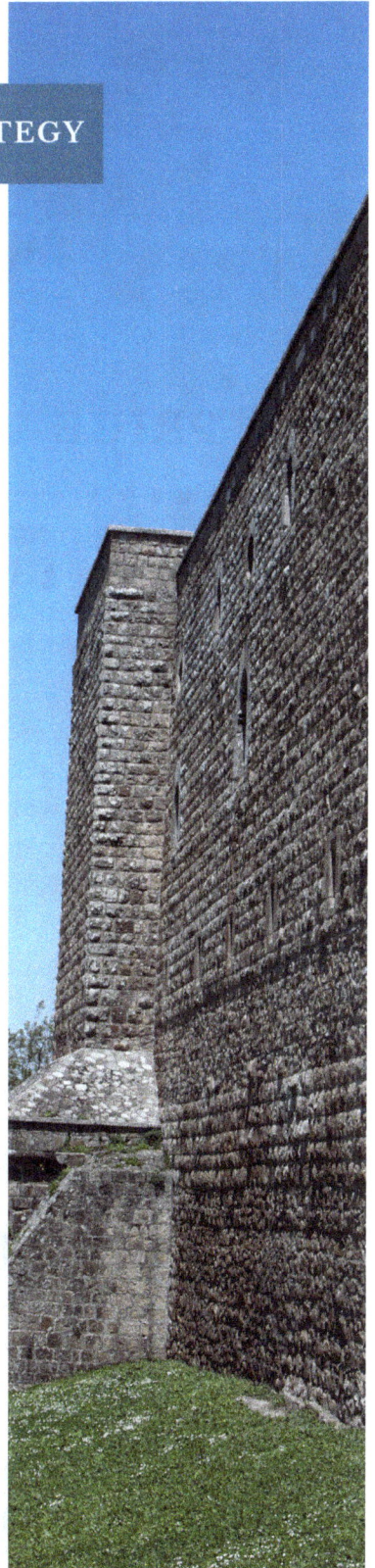

159.

"PRICE-TO-SALES RATIO"

This is a less common utilized metric to try to evaluate companies as compared with the more well known Price to Earnings ratio. It is often used with newer, less fully established companies that are in a hyper growth period of their life cycle but not earning much.

The Price to Sales Ratio calculates the price of a stock in relation to the annual sales that a company is generating. It works for newer, smaller companies best because those companies have not generated enough, or even any profits yet due to being in their early stage of development. The Price to Earnings ratio is the preferred metric for judging a company as ultimately earnings is what drives a stock price, not sales. But in the early stages of a company's life cycle, some metric is needed to analyze, and rationalize, stock prices.

160.

"HIGH WATER MARK"

A phrase generally tied to the fees one pays an investment advisor, High Water Mark is the highest level of value an account has reached. Oftentimes the fee paid to a Hedge Fund advisor is tied to this number if it's an account that pays fees tied to gains.

As an example: Let's say your stock account has reached $200,000. But then a stock market crash caused the account to lose 50%. The High Water Mark represents the amount the account must climb above before the Investor pays fees again on gains in the account. If the account climbs back to the original amount, from $100k back to $200k, the Investor pays no fees on this growth because it has not crossed the High Watermark previously achieved.

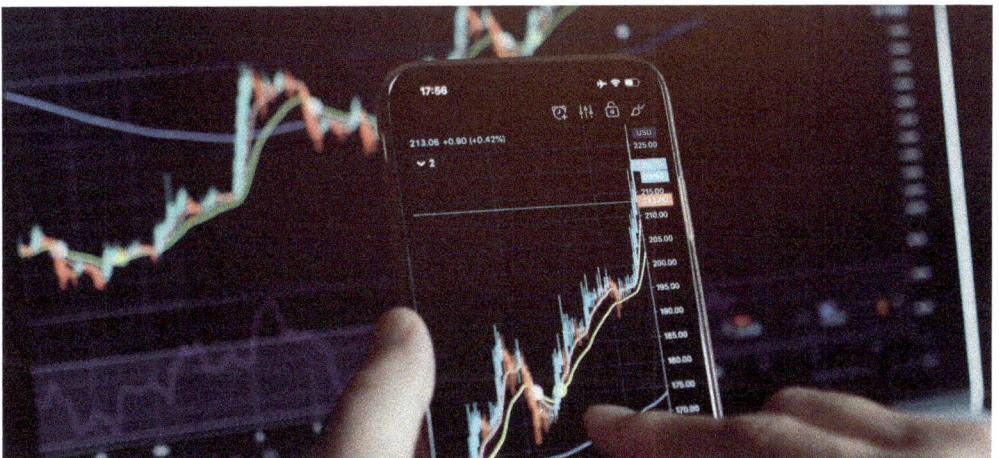

161.

"STOCK ROTATION"

This phrase concerns the movement of investment dollars from one category of stock assets to another. Most commonly, a stock rotation refers to the movement between Growth stocks and Value stocks, but it can also be the movement from Large capitalzation stocks to Small cap stocks.

In essence, many investment managers will move money from one sector of the stock market to another when they believe they will achieve greater returns in the future in the new category versus the old one. Often times investment managers act as a herd so many people move their investments at the same time and this seemingly coordinated movement is considered a Stock Rotation.

162.

"SOFT LANDING VS. HARD LANDING"

These terms are used in relation to how an economy acts when it slows down and perhaps crashes. A Hard Landing, in other words, means a painful recession that has led to substantial stock market losses as well as a large increase in unemployment due to layoffs and firings. Sometimes the Hard Landing feels like you fell through the floor.

A Soft Landing, which can include a very mild recession, usually includes no real recession at all, but merely a substantial slowing of an economy from the hypergrowth stage to slow or mild growth that is maintainable without Federal Reserve stimulus of decreasing interest rates.

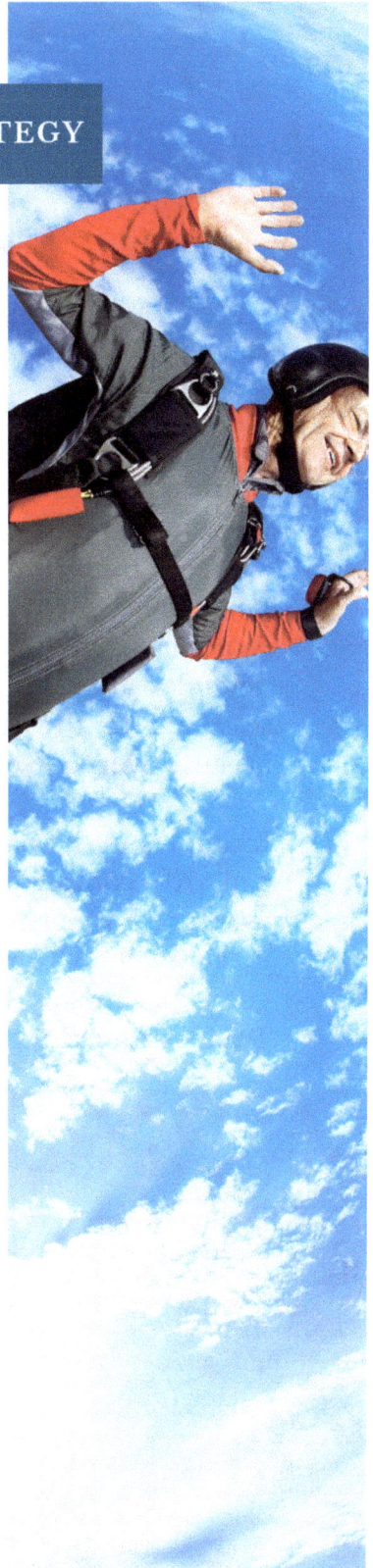

163.

"CROWDED TRADE"

Crowded Trade is a phrase that traders and stock analysts use quite often to describe certain Investments that have garnered too much attention, and more importantly, too much Investment dollars. Typically this happens when some investment, usually stocks but not always, is in the news day after day so that every investor from the most seasoned to the casual owns the asset. It's "crowded" because everyone owns it.

Examples in the past have been internet company stocks and AI company stocks. Unfortunately, there is eventually a reckoning because when a stock is crowded, it eventually becomes too overpriced irrespective of how good a company or investment it is. So a Crowded Trade is something to be aware of and be wary of.

164.

"INVESTMENT GRADE AND NON-INVESTMENT GRADE BONDS"

All bonds, be they corporate bonds or governmental bonds, are rated by Rating agencies such as Moody's and Standard and Poor's. Though the scales used by the rating agencies vary a bit, for the most part, they work on a letter-tiered system. The rating systems are designed to give an investor some sense of the risk of the Investment when one buys a bond.

All rating agencies have a risk line for which the bonds of companies above the line are considered less risky and higher classed, and those below the line which are considered much more risky and lower class. The higher-class bonds are called Investment Grade and the lower-class, more risky bonds are considered Non-Investment Grade.

165.

"THE DOW JONES INDICES"

While by far the most famous is the Dow Jones Industrial Average, which has expanded ludicrously its definition of what is an "industrial" stock, there are in fact more indices that exist. Like all Indices (the correct plural of 'index'), they are a small selection of stocks which hope to represent what is happening in a larger grouping.

For example, the famous Dow Jones Industrial Average has only 30 stocks in it. These specific 30 stocks have been chosen with the goal of representing the economy as a whole, though originally it was designed to represent the manufacturing industry more. Other important and much followed indices are the DJ Transportation Index and the DJ Utilities Index.

166.

"DOW THEORY"

Dow Theory is a concept among stock traders that suggests that the stock market is entering a bull market when two of the major Dow Jones indexes (the Dow Jones Industrial Average and the Dow Jones Transportation Average) reach new all-time highs.

In essence the reaching of new all-time highs in both indices represents a technical marker that traders feel comfortable represents the start or the signaling of a bull market. Given that the Dow Jones Industrial Average represents manufacturing and sales, and the Transportation Average represents the movement of goods around the country, there is some strong logic to the Dow Theory.

167.

"SEASONAL FACTORS

Many companies, and indeed the Investment market as a whole, is affected by what traders will call Seasonal Factors. These are reasons for why a company or the market are acting in a certain fashion dependant upon the season within the year.

Perhaps the most famous Seasonal Factor is the Christmas season as this can affect substantially the financial earnings of companies thus moving the market. Other Seasonal Factors can be the Summer months which will have less trading activity because traders go on vacation. This limited activity, driven by fewer people working, does have an effect on volumes and movements within the Investment markets. The famous stock market adage, "Sell in May and Go Away" is born of this phenomenon.

168.

"STRUCTURAL FACTORS"

In contrast to seasonal factors that are more temporary by definition, Structural Factors is a term used by Investment markets to capture elements that can drive investment market behavior over the long term. The term Structural implies that the Factor has the potential to be deeply rooted and sustainable.

Examples of Structural Factors are the state of the tax policies, long-term budgets and governmental deficits. These and many others affect this investment market over much longer periods of time than temporary seasonal factors. As a result, Structural Factors have a larger and longer lasting effect on investment prices and investor behavior and sentiments.

169.

"A BARBELL APPROACH / STRATEGY"

A Barbell Approach to investing is when an investor purchases what seems to be two opposing and somewhat contradictory ends of an investing strategy. The goal of this approach is to diversify returns in a tricky market environment.

For example: An investor can purchase very high risk stocks while at the same time also buying very conservative risk-free government bonds. By buying both ends of the risk spectrum with this Barbell Approach, the investor is trying to diversify themselves with exposure to different ends. There are endless ways of doing a Barbell Approach, the key factor is the buying of different ends of one investment strategy with the goal of protecting potential returns.

170.

"NET EXPENSE RATIO"

The Net Expense Ratio is the percentage in fees that an ETF or Mutual Fund manager charges the shareholders of the ETF or fund for managing it. It is measured as a percentage of the ETF or Fund's stock price.

For example, if the total Net Expense Ratio is listed as 2% for an ETF, the fund manager is charging 2% of the current price of the ETF in fees.

Net Expense Ratio is sometimes a useful metric by which to compare various funds as those funds with higher Net Expense Ratios need to generate greater returns to account for the higher expenses / fees they are charging the shareholder.

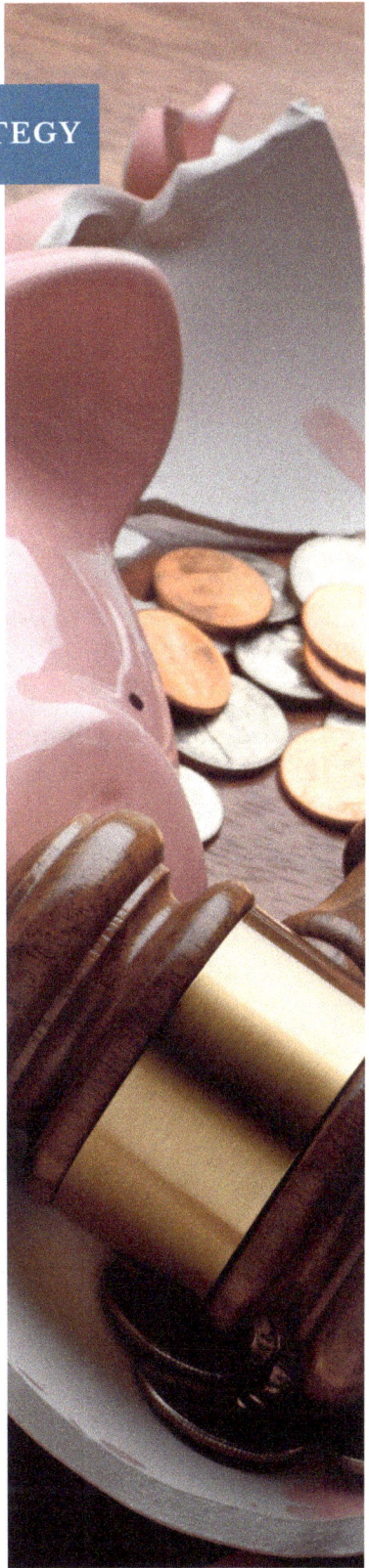

171.

"A STOCK PICKER'S MARKET"

An old saw that is often used in stock market investing is to call a period of time in the market a Stock Picker's Market. The implication is that the current market environment is one where it is better to buy individual stocks that you are "picking" specifically as opposed to purchasing broad index ETFs that capture the entire market as a whole.

In truth, it is always a Stock Picker's Market, as it is always a great time to find great companies and invest in them as Warren Buffett has shown. Additionally, it is important to remember that a broad base index mutual fund/ETF have generally generated greater returns than any stock picker over a long period of time. For the vast majority of investors, it is never a Stock Picker's Market as it is too hard to beat the overall average returns.

172.

"EXOGENOUS EVENTS"

Exogenous is a fancy word that means "something that came from outside of a system." Thus, an Exogenous Event is an event that occurs from outside of a system but affects the system substantially.

As pertains to investments, Exogenous Events are those that effect the stock or bond market, but are not directly internal to those markets. For example, a war breaking out in some important country. The war is not within the system of the investment markets, but its occurrence can have very outsized effects on the Investment markets. A pandemic is one. Trade war.

There are countless possible Exogenous Events that can affect investment markets, but sadly, it is nearly impossible to plan for them.

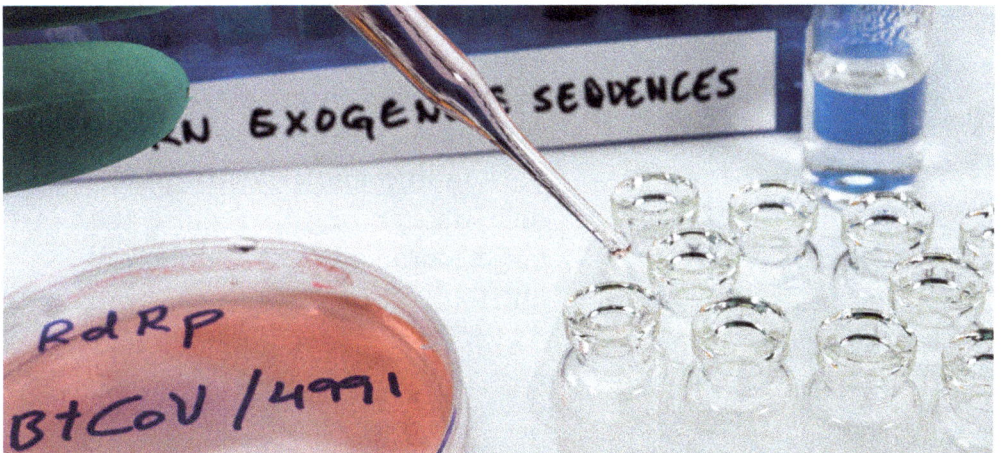

173.

"ENTERPRISE VALUE"

Enterprise Value is a lesser known, less utilized valuation of a company that includes the value of all the outstanding stock of the company plus the value of its outstanding net debt. Net debt is defined by the total value of bonds that are owed to the company's debt holders minus the total value of the cash and cash equivalents a company is holding.

Enterprise Value represents the total price that an acquiring company will have to pay to purchase the company they want to acquire. This is because the acquiring company will need to purchase all the shares outstanding and pay off all the debt outstanding to acquire the target company completely and outright.

174.

"TINA (THERE IS NO ALTERNATIVE)"

A phrase that grew in popularity in the early 2020s as interest rates plunged to his historically low levels, There Is No Alternative, or the acronym TINA, describes an investing environment where investors are forced to do one thing because there are no other good options.

Taking the 2020s as an example, interest rates were plunged to historically low levels as a function of the pandemic. Investors who wanted to generate some kind of return on their money had no alternative to stock market investing because one could not generate any decent return on Bond Market investing. There was no alternative so investors were forced into the stock market at a higher rate than usual.

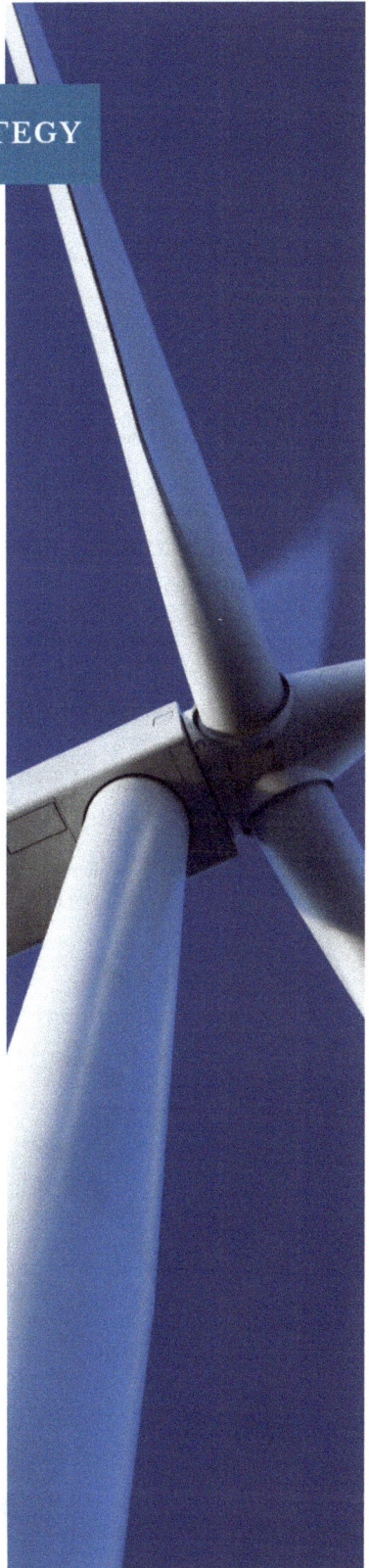

235

175.

"FUND/ETF BENCHMARKS"

Benchmarks in finance are things one can compare their asset against to analyze whether it is generating appropriate results. Similarly with investing, tracking against Benchmarks allow investors to track whether their investment is doing well compared to another similar investment.

Each Mutual Fund and ETF will have an appropriate benchmark, sometimes several, for which to compare against. It is essential to choose those that are extremely similar in nature because comparing apples and cars will not give the Investor any appropriate information. Though comparing against general benchmarks, like the S&P 500, may offer some generalized value.

176.

"ACTIVELY VS. PASSIVELY MANAGED FUND"

One of the many ways of understanding certain differences with mutual funds lies in how much trading the managers do in that fund. Funds are often categorized as being Actively or Passively Managed.

Passively Managed Funds are those that are tied very tightly to a specific index, and there is very little the fund manager deviates from that index, say perhaps the S&P500 or a Government Bond Index.

An Actively Managed Fund is one where the manager will buy and sell assets based on their belief and analysis with as much freedom and frequency as they think is appropriate to generate the best returns.

177.

"WASHOUT / SELLING CRESCENDO"

They're not something pretty, but they represent an incredible buying opportunity. A Washout or Selling Crescendo often but not always occur during a stock bear market and often they represent the final act in that bear market.

A Washout / Crescendo is when there is extreme selling of stocks, essentially panic selling as investors run for the exits at full speed. Historically each one is caused by some specific event that terrifies investors. In these instances the stock market may fall three to seven percent very quickly as all investors are trying to leave at the same time. For the courageous this is an opportunity.

178.

"LEVERAGED ETFS"

A very risky asset for purchase, Leveraged ETFs, are ETFs traded on an exchange that are tied to an index like other ETFs, but react at a multiple of what the associated underlying index returns.

For example, there is a Leveraged ETF tied to the S&P500 which will move 3 times what the S&P500 index does. So if on some very good day, the index goes up 1%, the Leveraged ETF will increase 3%. It is important to recognize the great risk involved with Leveraged ETFs because it is possible on a bad day for the S&P500 to drop 1% or even two to three times that. In this case, the Leveraged ETF could move three, four, five or even ten percent down negatively. Be very careful.

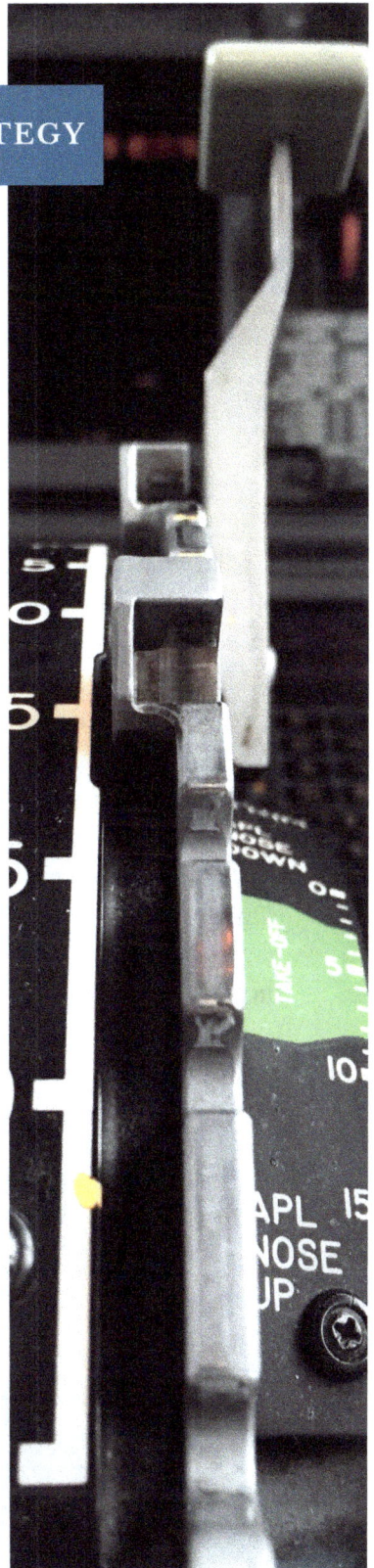

179.

"MOVING AVERAGES (50 DAY, 200 DAY, ETC.)

A major tool of Technical Analysis (defined elsewhere in the book), Moving Averages are calculations done on an investment, usually stock / ETFs. The calculations are the rolling average stock price over a period of time, most commonly 50 days or 200 days.

In essence, all the closing prices for a particular stock are added up based on a chosen time frame and then divided by that time frame in days (eg., 50 days) like any average. This generates a Moving Average over the 50 days and it can be continuously calculated and graphed as each new day the old drops off and the new is added. Stock investors often follow the 50-day and the 200-day Moving Averages on a daily basis searching for clues as to the next movement and the force of it.

180.

"PRICE ACTION"

Price Action is a term that seasoned traders investors use to describe the movement of an asset's price plotted over a period of time, be it one day, several weeks, or even over years. It is apical to all time lengths.

Let's say that Apple stock has price movement in a given day from $12.50 to $14.20. This movement of $1.80 from low to high is the Price Action. When can also review the price action over the month of September with a stock may have moved from $10.30 to $17.65. The movement from low to high in total, or vice versa, is known as the price action. What could say that the price action is very strong or weak depending on the range of the movement.

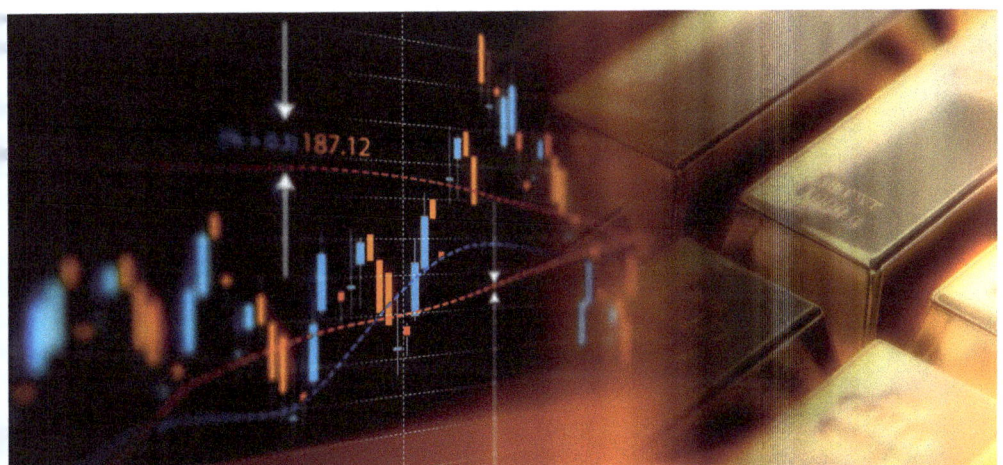

181.

"SUPPORT / RESISTANCE"

Essential Technical Analysis concepts, Support and Resistance are approximately opposite levels of buying or selling interest marked by a particular range of price points. They are imaginery defense points investors often take into account when making investing decisions.

An area of Support is a price range where buyers will come in and purchase the stock when it drops to that level, thereby 'supporting' the actual price. Conversely, an area of Resistance is a price range where investors will sell a stock if the price of the stock rises to the resistance level, creating resistance to it going higher. Both Support and Resistance act as temporary "physiological" barriers, and of course are not actual formalized barriers.

182.

"CONSOLIDATING / BASING"

It is extremely common that after a financial asset has made a substantial move, in either direction, it will enter a period of relative calm which results in essentially no movement in price. This period of relative 'flat-lining' is known in the markers as Consolidating or Basing.

In essence, the asset is building a base or consolidating it's recent moves, oftentimes as a precursor to it's next major move. However, it should be understood that the Basing period can be quite long, thus leaving the asset without much price movement for a substantial period of time. A long consolidation verifies the validity of the previous price movement.

243

183.

"RETRACEMENT / REVERSAL"

Essential terms in modern Technical Analysis, Retracement and Reversal speak to movement in an asset's price to a previous lower level after a rise higher, or vice versa, to a higher price after a move lower. It is the movement of returning to a previous state that mark a Retracement or a Reversal.

An example as the photo below demonstrates, the price has moved up sharply but after a good run higher, the asset's price reverses and retraces its path back to a lower state, a lower price point. These movements are very common, and used by traders to see if there is support for an asset at a certain price point.

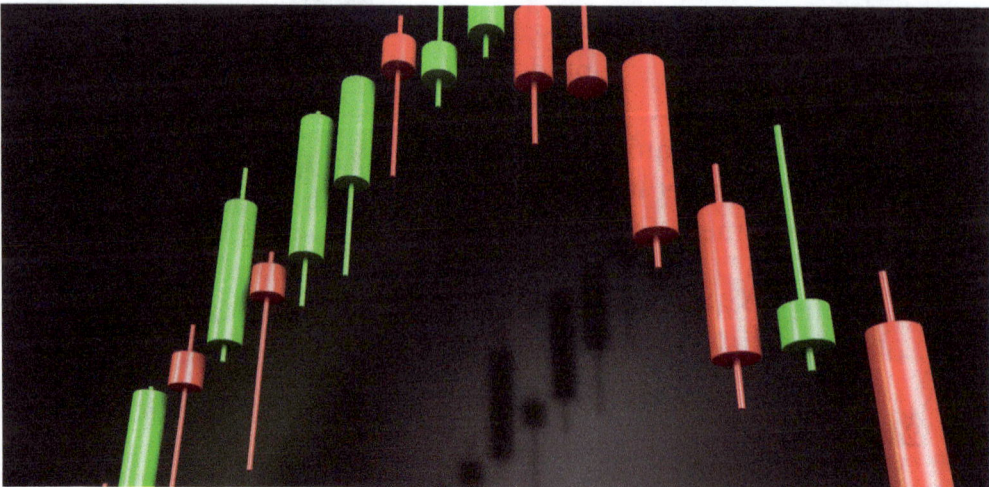

184.

"CORPORATE GUIDANCE (QUARTERLY)"

While in no way legally obligated to do so, almost all publicly traded companies give what is known as Corporate Guidance pertaining to their forecast for the coming quarter and often the coming year ahead. Since this happens on a quarterly basis it is often called Quarterly Guidance.

The quarterly Corporate Guidance will usually delivery forecasts for the upcoming quarter's expected revenue and earnings per share as well as it will usually forecast both of those metrics for the full year, and sometimes even for years to come. Wall Street followers this information is essential and highly anticipated and followed.

185.

"DEAD MONEY"

A painful, frustrating situation, Dead Money is when you have a stock that has not moved up over a long period of time while the overall stock market has moved up greatly. If a stock is up 1% over a five or ten year period, while the stock's sector or the general market has moved 7% a year compounded, it is said that the stock has been Dead Money.

It has happened to some of the greatest stocks over long periods in time including the entire biotech industry and stocks like Disney, Starbucks, and Apple. Sometimes analysts will make a prediction that a stock will be Dead Money as a way of saying the stock will vastly underperform its peers or the stock market as a whole. Look out for this in your holdings, and decide whether to move away from it.

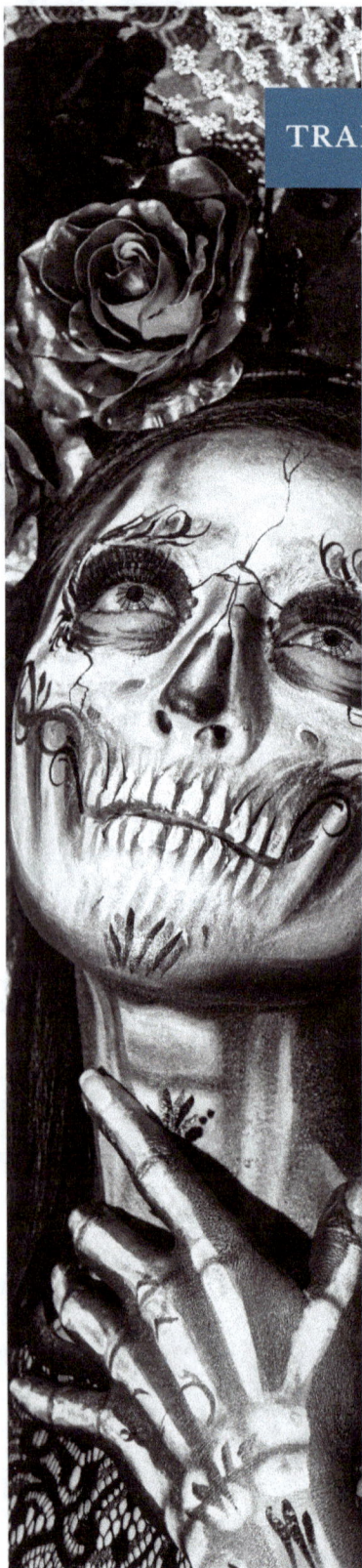

186.

"MARKET BREADTH"

Market Breadth refers to the concentration of stocks moving in a positive direction. The market is said to have breath when a large amount of stocks are moving in a positive direction. Poor Market Breadth is when only a very few amount of stocks are moving in a positive direction. Here, Market Breadth can be talked about in short periods like a day, or long periods over a month, quarter.

Good Market Breadth is usually a sign of health in the stock market. When positive stock movements are occurring in only very few stocks, and the vast majority are not moving positively, it is a sign of general weakness for the near-term future. The converse is true also, Good breadth augurs for a short-term positive future. Not always.

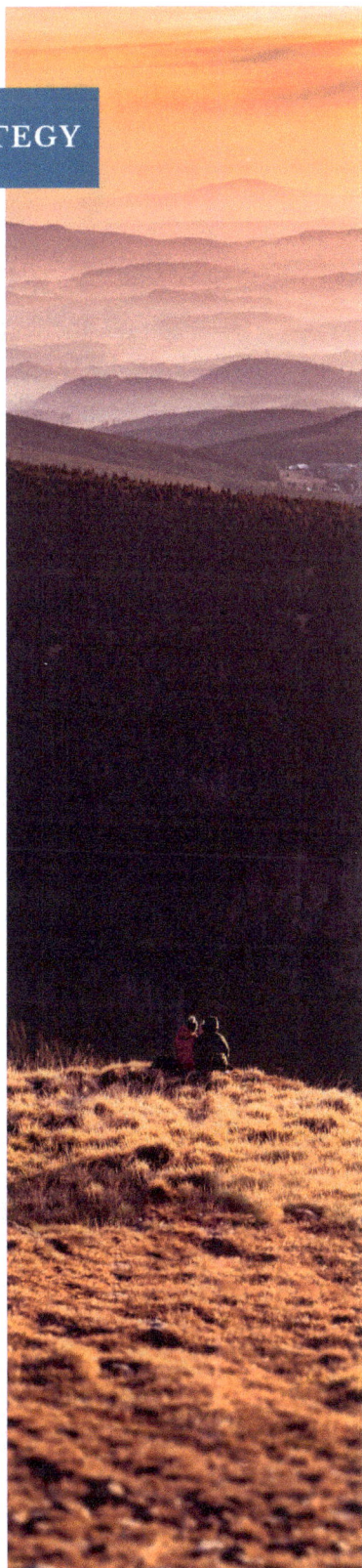

187.

"MOMENTUM / MOMENTUM STOCKS"

Investing in Momentum or Momentum Stocks is when an investor puts their money into stocks that have a consistent tendency to move strongly higher when the market is moving higher. In essence, these stocks ride the wave of a strong markey movement with greater force in the average market stock. We can say that someone is a Momentum investor when a high percentage of their investments is placed in stocks of this nature.

It is important to note the old investing adage that "what goes up fast often times comes down faster" and understand that there is great risk with substantial investments in Momentum.

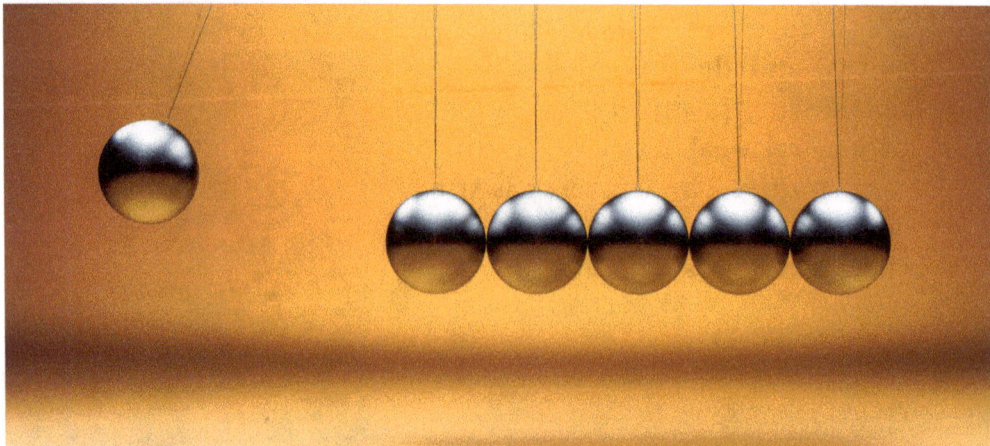

188.

"V BOTTOM"

A V Bottom, and sometimes talked about as a Hockey Stick bottom is when the stock market recovers from a sharp decline with an equally sharp rise in prices so that the movement in the stock market looks like a large V or the shape of a hockey stick.

V Bottoms happen surprisingly often, relatively, which is not to say they happen all the time or anywhere close to it. Given the nature of the stock market to overreact and overdo both its ups and downs, what's known as 'crescendo selling' often occurs at the end of a vicious down movement. When it does reverse strongly, the V Bottom is formed. It is a sign of strength for many as the large movement up shows investor interest as finally returned in a big way.

189.

"FREE CASH FLOW / FCF YIELD"

Free Cash Flow is a measure that captures the amount of money that a business has generated after all possible expenses and uses of cash have been removed. This includes all operating expenses, all taxes all investment dollars, all debt payments, all product purchases, everything. It is literally the cash that is left over that a company has for doing whatever it wants. The higher the number the healthier and more solvent the company is.

Free Cash Flow Yield is ratio of a company's free cash flow per share divided by its share price. Again, the greater the Free Cash Flow Yield, the greater the health of the company.

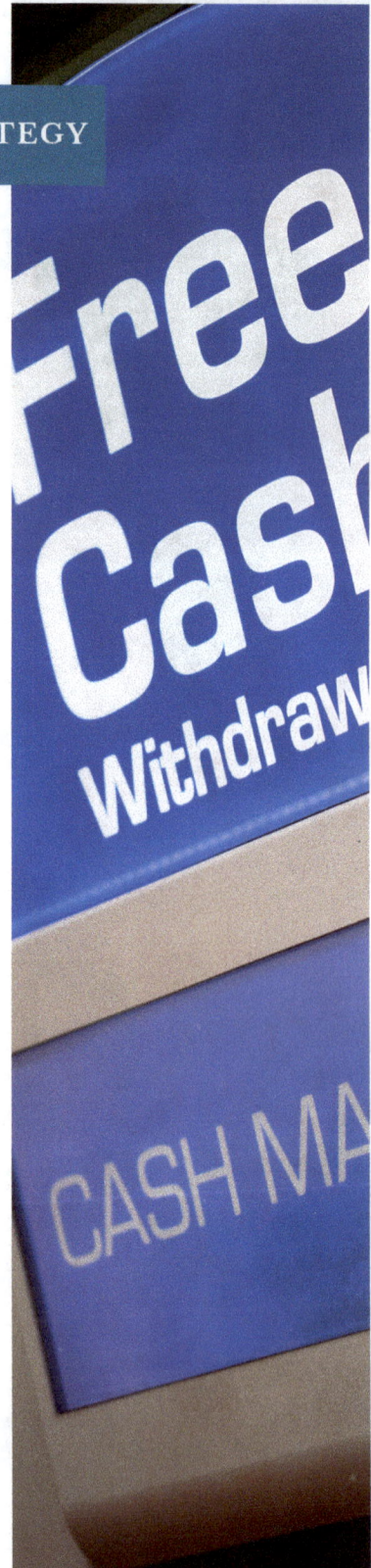

190.

"TRIPLE WITCHING HOUR"

This evocative term is not as scary as perhaps the name suggests, but it does lead to some very interesting Fridays. Each quarter on the 3rd Friday of the month the quarter ends (March, June, September, December), stock options, stock futures and related index options expire. Triple Witching Hour refers to that last hour of trading on that Friday.

Given the confluence of all these different options and futures expiring, there can be an incredible amount of stock trading activity on the final day and final hour, and sometimes related to it, substantial swings in either direction and sometimes even in both directions very quickly. Hold on tight.

191.

"ONE-TIME CHARGES"

Unlike the Christmas photo below, One-Time Charges not a gift for companies or investors. Partially an accounting term, but more specifically an item that investors consider, a One-Time Charge is a substantial cost or expense that a company incurs that materially affects their profitability. It comes in many forms, often perhaps a large legal settlement, or naturel disaster expense, or even a huge gambling loss in the case of casinos. There are myriad different types.

As investors, we tend to look past and mostly ignore One-time Charges as they by the nature are not recurring, and at their core, don't reflect what is going on with the company long term.

192.

"WHALE WATCHING"

This is a cute phrase that has developed in recent years to describe how the investing market follows what very large, historically-successful investors are doing. A "Whale" in this instance, is name used to describe these giant investors like Warren Buffett for example.

Whale Watching is following how these specific investors are changing their investments from quarter to quarter. Giant investors of this type have to make formal filings with the government about their large investments. Many in the investing public will research what they have bought and sold and make similar decisions accordingly. That is, buying selling what they bought and sold. Whale decisions do move the market the next day.

193.

"13-F FILINGS"

Related to Whale Watching, 13F Filings are legal disclosure filings that all hedge funds and other investment management firms of all sorts must file with the SEC each quarter. The filing details all the major holdings of the fund on a stock by stock basis. The disclosures are made 45 days after the quarter ends.

For certain very high-profile investors, the 13F Filings are essential reading to see what changes have occured in the investor's holding, what's been sold and what's been bought. It's important to remember that the Filings become public 45 days after the filing, and during that time, theoretically, countless changes could have occurred. Thus the filing must be taken analyzed certain amount of caution.

254

194.

"QUARTERLY REBALANCING"

A large chunk of stock market indexes are what's known as Market Capitalization weighted, meaning the index is affected by the larger companies in the index more than the smaller companies. This is as opposed to Equal Capitalization weighted indexes, where each stock is an equal percentage of the index.

With Market Cap weighted indexes, there is a Quarterly Rebalancing of the percentages each stock is of the index to reflect the movement in the stock price during the quarter. and thus the waiting of each stock in the index. These quarterly rebalancings happen on the third Friday of each quarter ends month (March, June, etc.) and can affect the price of the index in a meaningful way depending on stock price movements of the larger cap companies.

195.

"SANTA CLAUS RALLY"

A rather surprisingly consistent phenomenon that happens often, the Santa Claus rally, as the name suggests, happens in late December and early January and results in the stock market making very solid gains during this period. On average, stocks will make 1-2% gains during this 7-10 day period as measured by the major indexes S&P 500 and NASDAQ.

In general, mid to the end of December is very often one of the best periods for the stock market each year, and many people think of this period as part of the Santa Claus rally as well. It is important to know that the rally is not absolute or guaranteed, and does not always happen but more like four out of five years.

196.

"GAPPING / GAPPING UP OR DOWN"

Usually stocks trade consistently in consecutive time periods, with the end of one period leading into the beginning of the next period. If Apple stock closes Monday's session at $200, it usually opens Tuesday's session somewhere nearby that.

Gapping, which can be in either direction up or down, is when a stock substantially moves between two consecutive time periods: It closed at $200 and opened at $220 or $180. These substantial swings represent the fact that something has occurred to cause a dramatic shift in the price action of the asset. Big news items, earnings releases can often be a factor to cause a gapping.

ABOUT THE AUTHOR

Mr. Goldstein is currently the President and Founder of Goldart Consulting LLC, a Small Business consulting firm specializing in marketing, finance, strategy & management consulting to micro and small businesses, start-up operation. Current and past clients are based throughout America, as well as in many countries in Europe and Asia. He has helped Small Businesses generate many millions in revenue and profits.

Previously, as the Director of Financial Planning and Analysis at SFX Entertainment Inc., a forerunner to Live Nation Inc., Mr. Goldstein helped analyze and complete over $3 billion in Merger and Acquisition activity including the acquisition of the industry's leading concert promoters and entertainment companies such as Bill Graham Presents, PACE Entertainment, Contemporary Productions, Don Law, & David Falk Mgmt.

Prior to this, Mr. Goldstein was the Manager of Strategic Planning in Corporate Sales and Marketing at Cablevision Systems, then the country's fifth largest cable system and owner of several Entertainment assets including the Madison Square Garden, Radio City Music Hall, the New York Knicks and Rangers, and the American Movie Classics and Bravo television channels.

Mr. Goldstein has a Masters of Business Administration in Finance from New York University and a Bachelor of Science in Management in Marketing from Tulane University in New Orleans.

258

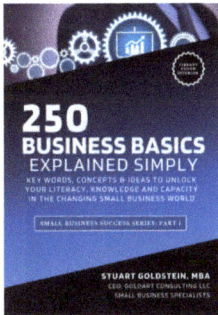

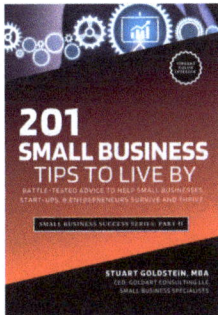

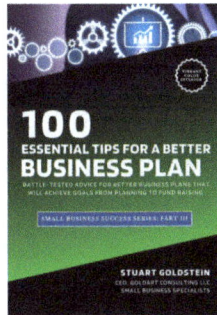

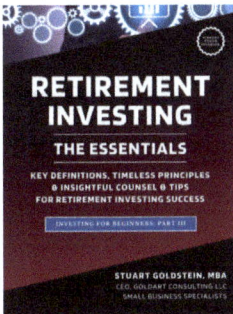

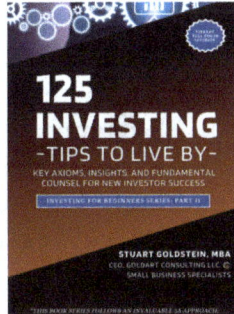

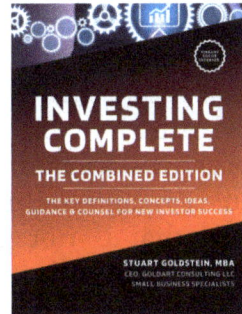

THANK YOUS & ACKNOWLEDGEMENTS

I would like to thank enormously the following, which helped make this endeavor possible and cost effective:

CANVA SOFTWARE: This is an incredible software program and application that allows one to build graphic projects such as this book. The paid-tier is even better as it allows you a ton of free photos for use.

PIXABAY: This is a magnificent site allows you to download free photos for use in products such as this.

Thank you to my many clients over the years, who have been the sounding board and on the receiving end of these "Tips" as I created and refined them.

ABOUT THE PUBLISHER: GOLDART PUBLISHING LLC

Goldart Publishing LLC is a sister company of Goldart Consulting LLC is a Small Business Consulting practice specializing in Finance, Marketing, Strategic Planning and Management. It was started 22 years ago with the goal of bringing the latest in Enterprise advisory, the skills, practices and efforts oftentimes the difference between success and failure, to Small Businesses companies at a cost that is not prohibitive. Over these years, we have helped countless Enterprises in myriad industries and countries accomplish the goals they've set out to achieve.

Please feel free to contact us if you need
help with your Small or Mid-sized Business
Goldart Consulting LLC
(888) 203 -6419
www.goldartcconsulting.com

www.ingramcontent.com/pod-product-compliance
Lightning Source LLC
Chambersburg PA
CBHW061207220326
41597CB00015BA/1545